THE OFFICIAL High Times
POT SMOKER'S HANDBOOK

THE OFFICIAL
High Times
POT SMOKER'S HANDBOOK

FEATURING 420 THINGS TO DO WHEN YOU'RE STONED

By David Bienenstock and the editors of *High Times* magazine

CHRONICLE BOOKS
SAN FRANCISCO

DEDICATION

🌿 Tom Forcade founded *High Times* in 1974 while in the middle of a highly lucrative career as a marijuana smuggler and dealer. Much like his day job, Forcade got into publishing for the adventure, the hustle, the thrill (and the money, too)—but mainly because he believed strongly in marijuana and the people who smoke it.

For Forcade, launching *High Times* represented only one act in a lifetime of activism, both overt and covert, and always subversive. See page 30 for a biography of Tom Forcade, including the full story on the Hippie Mafia, the Underground Press Syndicate, planeloads of Colombian weed, dealers who use forklifts, and the seeds that started a revolutionary magazine.

Page 208 constitutes a continuation of the copyright page.

Library of Congress Cataloging-in-Publication Data:
Bienenstock, David.
   The official High times pot smoker's handbook :
featuring 420 things to do when you're stoned /
by David Bienenstock and the editors of High Times
magazine.
     p. cm.
  ISBN 978-0-8118-6205-9
  1. Marijuana. 2. Marijuana abuse. 3. Drugs. 4. Drug
abuse. I. High times. II. Title.
HV5822.M3B46 2008
306'.1—dc22

2008022905

Manufactured in China
Designed by Laura Bagnato

10 9 8 7 6 5 4 3 2

Chronicle Books LLC
680 Second Street
San Francisco, CA 94107
www.chroniclebooks.com

CONTENTS

Chapter 1

HIGHSTORY

So, you've started smoking pot . . . or perhaps you've been burning down since the '60s and just picked up this handbook to see if there's anything new under the stoned sun. In either case—or anywhere in between—you can rest assured that you're in highly distinguished company: Astronomer Carl Sagan embarked upon his most mind-bending insights into the cosmos while baked off his ass. Louis Armstrong, the exalted inventor of modern jazz, burned reefers on the daily—three cigar-sized joints per day. And when self-made billionaire Michael Bloomberg, one of the most success-ful businessmen in the world, was asked during his winning campaign for mayor of New York if he'd ever inhaled marijuana, he famously replied, "You bet I did. And I enjoyed it."

So there you have it: Toking the herb won't prevent you from reaching the highest levels of achievement in academia, the arts, science, business, or government. On the other hand, you must take (and pass!) a drug test to land a job behind the counter at Blockbuster Video. Of course, that sad irony has a lot to do with Wayne Huizenga—"Cockbuster" founder, Miami Dolphins owner, censorship supporter, and major player in the $7-billion-per-year drug-test industry. And speaking of irony: Wayne must have been a little *pissed* in 2004, when Ricky Williams, the Dolphins' star running back, failed a urine test and subsequently fled the country before announcing an early retirement. "I didn't quit football because I failed a drug test," Williams told the *Miami Herald*, admitting that he'd previously used a masking agent to hide his devotion to cannabis. "I failed a drug test because I was ready to quit football."

Williams sat out for a year (the Dolphins finished in last place), briefly returned to the NFL, and then decided to join the Canadian Football League, where his love of natural grass would be more easily accepted. "It's just a plant. It's a seed—you throw it in the ground and it grows," the Pro Bowl back explained upon reporting for duty with the Toronto Argonauts. "And people in my country, they trip about it."

(If *you're* facing a drug test any time in the near future, please feel free to skip ahead to page 64 now.)

❦ EVERYBODY MUST GET STONED

As for the rest of us, a quick *highstory* lesson seems to be in order. After all, we truly smoke on the shoulders of giants—our torch has been passed down from Chinese herbalists, Islamic hashish eaters, African herbsmen, Jamaican rastas, Pancho Villa's Mexican revolutionaries, and New Orleans' legendary jazz-cats to beatniks, hippies, yippies, punks, ravers, and hip-hoppers, and now on to a new generation of modern stoners, scattered like seeds across the earth, but globally connected by a common philosophy, an underground etiquette, and the ongoing struggle to free the weed. Everywhere in the world, marijuana has been misunderstood and maligned by the mainstream, treated as anything from a nuisance to a capital crime. And yet in all of these places, a rebel force exists dedicated to growing, smoking, and sharing this most wondrous and benign plant, whatever the risk. *Vive la résistance!*

Pot people may be an oppressed minority, but we still know how to party, whether it's crowds of 250,000 at the annual Hempfest in Seattle or just a few old friends passing a joint in the parking lot behind the bowling alley. Pot people love music, food, art, dancing, movies, sex, hikes, skinny-dips, silly jokes, campfires, and long soul-searching conversations—all of which can be wonderfully enhanced by getting high. Pot people are also peaceful, open, honest, funny, creative, humble, and inclusive. That's not to say that every *individual* who smokes pot shares these characteristics—far from it, dude—but marijuana culture, taken as a whole, has flowered into an alternative universe we should all feel proud to inhabit. *We're here, we're stoned, get used to it*—and may we all be blessed enough to someday wake up in a world where the herbalists have been put in charge. Until then, let's agree up front not to get caught.

Now, on to our highstory lesson: Humanity's long, often dysfunctional relationship with *Cannabis sativa* dates back to at least 6000 B.C., when the Chinese first discovered hemp seeds as a food source. This excellent and nutritious snack is available today in America's health food stores, despite an all-out ban on growing domestic hemp—the THC-deficient cousin of kind buds that looks like marijuana, but smokes like rope (see "Hemp, Hemp, Hooray," page 188).

"No court has specifically ruled that a live cannabis plant is a non-controlled substance or that farming these plants is not a regulated activity," Governor Arnold Schwarzenegger wrote in a 2006 statement vetoing a California bill to legalize hemp farming. "As a result, it would be improper to approve a measure that directly conflicts with current federal statutes and court decisions," he argued, sounding a bit like one of the "girly men" he typically pummels on the big screen.

Wouldn't want to be *improper*, huh Arnold? Good thing we've got a real action hero like you to protect us, although just north of the border, Canadians make nice livings growing hemp—not only for food, but also for fiber and fuel—while America has the shameful distinction of watching its family farmers go broke in a country suffering an obesity crisis. Oh, and don't forget, marijuana, the nation's #1 cash crop, is also banned, creating an estimated $40 billion black market of untaxed, unregulated income for farmers of a more illicit disposition.

(If *you've* already decided to grow your own, whether as a hobby, head stash, for medicine, or for profit, feel free to skip ahead to page 177.)

The Chinese, who caught on to the benefits of cannabis early, also provide the first evidence of hemp clothing (4000 B.C.) and medical marijuana (2727 B.C.). Cannabis's medicinal properties owe their discovery to Emperor Shennong, also known as "The Divine Farmer," revered for teaching both agriculture and medicine in ancient China. Legend has it that Emperor Shennong took it upon himself

Wild cannabis grows near the Altai Mountains in western China, possibly the birthplace of the first marijuana plants on Earth.

to personally taste hundreds of wild herbs to test for their healing properties, discovering 365 medicines and a few poisonous plants along the way. The results were published in *The Divine Farmer's Herb-Root Classic*, which included a flowery passage recommending cannabis as a "superior" treatment for "constipation, 'female weakness,' gout, malaria, rheumatism, and absentmindedness."

Now, almost five thousand years later, we live in a culture that breathlessly advertises beer and hard-on pills during Sunday afternoon baseball games, but denies the sick and dying access to a healing herb. When the issue of medical marijuana reached the U.S. Supreme Court in 2005 in

Hindu deity Shiva mixes up a batch of bhang, *a Cannabis concoction popular in India since at least 1200 B.C.*

Gonzalez v. Raich, the majority ruled that a chronically ill woman, living in a state that had legalized medical use of marijuana, who was growing her own plant on her own property for her own personal consumption on doctor's orders in order to save her own life, was somehow engaged in "interstate commerce."

And so a supposedly conservative court, allegedly interested in upholding the ideal of "state's rights," justified invoking the Interstate Commerce Clause of the Constitution to defend the federal government's policy of entering California and enforcing the Controlled Substances Act—i.e., arresting Angel Raich, who suffered from an inoperable brain tumor at the time of the trial (see "Supreme Disappointment," page 159).

Twelve states have approved medical marijuana laws so far, and while the Feds occasionally meddle, more states will certainly join the list as voters increasingly express their preference for common sense and compassion over a heartless, ineffective, and never-ending War on Some Drugs and Some of the People Who Use Them.

(If you or someone you love needs medical marijuana, or if you want to learn more about the struggle for safe access to this medicinal plant, please see page 151.)

Well, that briefly covers the body and mind, but what about the soul? The earliest records of spiritual marijuana use pertain to *bhang*, or "sacred grass," an Indian cannabis drink praised for "releasing anxiety" in the Atharvaveda, one of the four vedas comprising the oldest scriptural Hindu texts. Since around 1200 B.C., *bhang*—a warm blend of milk, almonds, fresh buds, and spices—has been consumed as an offering to Lord Shiva, and the concoction remains widely available today, despite India's official ban on marijuana. *Bhang* is associated in particular with the playful Hindu spring festival Holi, which commemorates a tale in Hindu religious mythology. (If you can't make it to India this spring, and you want to see what you're missing, simply flip to our drink recipe, "More Bhang for Your Buck," on page 63. While you're there, check out our staff's favorite ganja foods, but be sure to carefully monitor your dosage. When it comes to eating your weedies, too much of a good thing can be, well, *too much*. Not to mention *far out*.)

As for marijuana's notorious role as an aphrodisiac, we can confirm that phenomenon at least as far back as 500 B.C., the date archeologists ascribed to a grave site discovered in Kazakhstan where a pair of Scythian lovers had been buried together, along with a leather pouch containing wild marijuana seeds. Countless cannabis couples have come along since, and while an equally countless amount of informal research and anecdotal evidence shows that smoking a spliff both before and after sex can be fantastic, the same evidence also indicates that smoking one *during* sex can be difficult to downright dangerous.

Of course, the combination of sex and drugs (not to mention rock and roll) doesn't exactly appeal to everyone equally, particularly those not partaking in either. Or, as Dr. Timothy Leary famously put it: "Psychedelic drugs cause paranoia, confusion, and total loss of reality in politicians that have never taken them." For example, in his

Acid guru Timothy Leary grooved on grass, too, even when seeking higher office.

crusade against cannabis in the 1930s, Harry J. Anslinger, commissioner of the Federal Bureau of Narcotics, portrayed pot as a sexual menace, inventing fantastic descriptions of reefer–crazed Negroes seducing white women with devil weed. Anslinger used these lurid tales to scare the populace into compliance with his war on "marihuana," which he also linked to America's recent influx of Mexican immigrants.

Anslinger even went old school, citing stories of drug-crazed terrorists who ran amok in the 12th century as evidence of marijuana's sinister nature. This tall tale, attributed to Marco Polo after his return from Persia, tells of the infamous *hashshashin*, a secret mystical Islamic sect controlled by Al-Hassan ibn al-Sabbah—a powerful warlord who commanded an elite band of Shi'ite warriors dedicated to overthrowing the existing order through a series of daring political killings, usually executed by dagger in daylight. The *hashshashin* became so notoriously proficient at this sort of attack that they gave rise to a new word—*assassin*.

That's the history. As for the legend, al-Sabbah would find likely candidates for his fighting forces and feed them enough hashish to either lose consciousness or enter a waking dream. While under this spell, the initiates would be transported to a secret garden hidden inside the walls of a castle, where actors playing ghosts would rouse them with graphic descriptions of the eternal delights awaiting those who die in the service of Allah and al-Sabbah. A number of beautiful women would then appear in the lush garden—willing partners called *houris* in Arabic—and offer themselves up to the *hashshashin*-in-training. During orgiastic lovemaking sessions that would last for hours, these women would whisper promises of the exponentially more overwhelming delights awaiting these young men in paradise, should they die as martyrs in the field of battle. By the next morning, another fearless and loyal *hashshashin* warrior would be born—not only willing, but eager to fight

and die in the name of Allah after having been shown the open doors to paradise.

So, yeah . . . uh-huh, that sort of thing happens every day. Anyway, if you think the great pot debate has gotten any more reasonable in the last seventy years, here's what John Walters, George W. Bush's "Drug Czar," had to say about the great green menace: "Marijuana today is a much more serious problem than the vast majority of Americans understand." *Really?* How serious can it be if the vast majority of Americans don't think it's a problem?

In 1799, Napoleonic soldiers returning from Egypt brought the first hashish to Europe, establishing an eager market that's existed ever since, although both Napoleon and Pope Innocent VIII attempted to ban its use. By the 1840s, cannabis-based medicines were widely available in American drug stores, and in Paris, *Le Club des Hachichin* ("The Hashish Eater's Club"; 1844–1849), dedicated to exploring drug-induced experiences, attracted such French writers and intellectuals as Alexandre Dumas, *père*, Victor Hugo, Charles Baudelaire, and Théophile Gautier.

Noting this increasing consumption in Europe and the United States, in 1893 the British government, then ruling India, established the Indian Hemp Commission to investigate the use of cannabis in the country. After consulting with more than 1,200 "doctors, coolies, yogis, fakirs, heads of lunatic asylums, bhang peasants, tax gatherers, smugglers, army officers, hemp dealers, ganja palace operators, and the clergy," the Commission concluded in its 3,281-page report, the most comprehensive, scientific study ever undertaken of the herb, that "for the vast majority of consumers . . . the evidence shows the moderate use of ganja or *charas* not to be appreciably harmful . . ."

October 2, 1937 Want a second, more recent opinion? In 1988, Drug Enforcement Administration (DEA) Law Judge Francis L. Young prepared a report in response to a petition by the National Organization for the Reform of Marijuana Laws (NORML) seeking to reschedule cannabis, then (and now) a Schedule 1 substance—the most restrictive category, reserved for drugs such as heroin and crack, which cause great harm and have no medicinal value. Young's report, which (unsuccessfully) argued in favor of rescheduling, concluded rather unambiguously that "Marijuana is the safest therapeutically active substance known to man . . . safer than many foods we commonly consume."

Yet despite the ever-growing mountain of empirical evidence in support of loosening regulation of marijuana, those in control of the government have almost always gone the other way, manipulating public opinion in order to create increasingly harsh policies on cannabis, starting in 1933, when America's brief and disastrous experiment with alcohol prohibition finally ended and a lot of newly created law enforcement officers stood to lose their jobs. Four propaganda-filled years later, Congress approved the Marihuana Tax Stamp Act of 1937, which didn't make marijuana illegal so much as levy taxes on its sale so high that nobody could afford to legally sell it. Harry

The 1937 mug shot of Samuel R. Caldwell, the first American arrested in the War on Marijuana.

Anslinger urged the Act's passage on the grounds that grass caused "murder, insanity, and death."

On October 2, 1937—the very day the law was enacted—a 58-year-old unemployed laborer and

part-time reeferman named Samuel R. Caldwell set up shop in Denver's seedy Lexington Hotel. Local police and FBI officers raided, caught Caldwell in the act of selling two joints, and took him down for dealing—the first person ever charged under the brand-new federal law. Judge Foster Symes, who presided at Caldwell's trial, must have been getting his "fair and balanced" news on marijuana from William Randolph Hearst, the dean of yellow journalism, whose numerous newspapers relentlessly published headlines like *"MARIJUANA MAKES FIENDS OF BOYS IN 30 DAYS"* and *"HASIESH* [sic] *GOADS USERS TO BLOOD LUST."*

"I consider marijuana the worst of all narcotics, far worse than the use of morphine or cocaine. Under its influence men become beasts," Judge Symes declared, sentencing Caldwell to four years of hard labor. "I have no sympathy with those who sell this weed. The government is going to enforce this new law to the letter."

Samuel R. Caldwell served every day of his sentence in Leavenworth Penitentiary, on top of a $1,000 fine, and died a year after his release. He represents the first prisoner of war in the War on Marijuana, which, like any important military campaign, was preceded by a coordinated propaganda campaign of blatant disinformation designed to lay the groundwork for victory.

The Hempire Strikes Back And so, Hearst's paranoid headlines found reinforcement in books such as *Reefer Club* and movies like *Marijuana: Assassin of Youth* and *The Road to Ruin*. Just a year before the Marijuana Tax Stamp Act passed, the most laughable of these efforts, *Reefer Madness*—a church-financed educational film purchased by a sensationalist producer and sold on the exploitation circuit—depicted a world in which one puff led to instant insanity. The film languished in obscurity until it was rediscovered in the Library of Congress in 1971 by NORML founder Keith Stroup, who promptly bought a print and took it with him on a college tour to raise money for his then-fledgling organization, one of the first ever dedicated to the cause of marijuana legalization.

NORML would also receive major help in its early years from *Fear and Loathing in Las Vegas* author Hunter S. Thompson, whom Stroup first encountered smoking a joint under the bleachers at the 1971 Democratic National Assembly in Miami; Hugh Hefner, who'd previously extolled the virtues of marijuana as part of his *Playboy* philosophy; and *High Times* founder Tom Forcade, who once anonymously left $10,000 in cash on NORML's Washington, D.C., doorstep, crediting the gift to "The Confederation," a fictitious group of growers and smugglers he hoped would inspire other "high rollers" to tithe back into the marijuana movement.

NORML still fights for marijuana legalization today, joined by a growing and varied community of drug law reformers, including two of the newest organizations to spring up in solidarity, which have turned unique perspectives on this issue into rapidly growing movements for social and political change.

In 1998, Representative Mark Souder (R-Indiana) added an amendment to the Higher Education Act (HEA) denying federal financial aid to anyone with a drug conviction, including simple pot possession (murderers and arsonists still welcome, though). This senseless drug policy, dubbed the "Aid Elimination Penalty" by student activists, inspired the formation of Students for Sensible Drug Policy (SSDP). After eight years of advocacy, the organization finally convinced Congress to partially rescind the penalty, rewriting the amendment so it only applies to those busted while *currently* receiving aid, not to those pinched in the past. Since tens of thousands of students may still lose federal aid this year, SSDP now pushes for passage of the Removing Impediments to Students' Education Act, which would eliminate the Aid Elimination Penalty entirely. One of the fastest-growing student organizations in America, with chapters on more than seventy five college campuses, SSDP has expanded to oppose the entire War on Drugs, a mission reflected in their motto: "Schools, not prisons."

Safer Alternative For Enjoyable Recreation (SAFER) was formed in 2005 after several students overdosed on alcohol on college campuses in Colorado. SAFER promotes the idea that marijuana represents a safer recreational alternative to drinking, and should be treated equivalently by both lawmakers and college administrations. Focusing on this alcohol–marijuana comparison, SAFER helped pass a citywide ballot initiative in Denver that legalized up to an ounce of herb for personal adult use, and went on to sponsor a similar effort for the entire state of Colorado that earned 40 percent of the vote.

NORML, SSDP, SAFER, and other organizations (see page 152) fighting back in the War on Marijuana need your help. Remember, getting involved in activism not only helps the cause, it's also a great way to get connected to the cannabis community—kind people, with a common interest, working to preserve our freedom. What could be better?

Paranoia Will Destroy Ya Unfortunately, these efforts face increasingly sophisticated and well-funded opposition from the Office of National Drug Control Policy (ONDCP) and the "Drug Czar," which, not satisfied with spending billions to arrest and incarcerate pot smokers every year, sank an additional $120 million in 2007 into an insidious advertising campaign designed to convince people to obey the marijuana laws. This incredibly costly and pervasive propaganda program predictably never questioned whether the need for these ads indicates the existence of bad laws in the first place.

Both the Office of Budget Management and the National Institute on Drug Abuse have studied the infamous ONDCP ads—which send such mixed and misleading messages as "smoking pot will cause you to kill small children" and "smoking pot will make you melt into the couch in unbearable apathy"—and found that not only are they ineffective at keeping kids off marijuana, but they may have the opposite effect. Much like *Reefer Madness* before them, these ads, along with the '80s classic "This is your brain on drugs," will someday serve as kitschy nostalgia for the future stoners of America. But even reconsidered as entertainment, $120 million seems like an awfully big budget. After all, the *Reefer Madness* print

Sensationalistic books and exploitation movies served as vital propaganda tools for scaring the populace into compliance with pot prohibition.

11
hopped-up killer against a city.
MARIHUANA
OMPLETE
AND
ABRIDGED

Keith Stroup bought for NORML only cost $297, and the ensuing sales of the film grossed enough money to get New Line Cinema off the ground (the giant Hollywood studio behind the *Lord of the Rings* trilogy and *Harold and Kumar Go to White Castle*).

Back in 1972, just two years after Keith Stroup founded NORML, Richard Nixon appointed a bipartisan panel, the National Commission on Marijuana and Drug Abuse, to study marijuana. Nixon had first envisioned America's modern War on Drugs during a 1968 presidential campaign speech he gave at Disneyland in which he identified narcotics as the nation's #1 domestic problem and promised aggressive solutions. After his hand-picked experts studied marijuana and subsequently recommended that personal use should be decriminalized, Tricky Dick roundly rejected their report, recognizing that harsh marijuana laws could be an effective tool against the growing antiwar counterculture and other so-called subversive elements.

Of course, that's just paraphrasing the prez. To be fair, let's let Nixon have the last word in his own words, which were fortunately caught on tape in the White House: "Do you think the Russians allow dope? Hell, no. Not if they can catch it, they send them up. You see, homosexuality, dope . . . uh, immorality in general—these are the enemies of strong societies. That's why the Communists and the left-wingers are pushing it. They're trying to destroy us." And they say *smoking* pot makes you paranoid. Anyway, a year after rejecting the findings of his Commission, Nixon created the Drug Enforcement Administration (DEA) instead.

Friends in High Places A year after that, in 1974, Tom Forcade launched *High Times* magazine to provide counterintelligence to those of us trying to survive on the outlaw side of this new kind of war. In addition to pot photography, cultural coverage, and political advocacy, a copy of *High Times* could provide the name of a friendly lawyer in your home state or the price of a kilo of hash in Kabul, Afghanistan—invaluable information to those in need of it in a time long before the Internet.

Richard Nixon knows good dope.

"A little knowledge goes a long way when prospecting for a good buy," *HT* issue #1 advised would-be cannabis consumers. "Prices may seem high and a dealer's rap about grades of grass can become confusing, but when you investigate the qualitative differences involved and the hassles it took to get that weed to your living room, it's easier to make accommodations."

A pot smuggler in the glory days, when it meant piloting light planes from Colombia to remote landing strips in the Florida Everglades—flying low, under the radar—Tom Forcade understood that a truly free press was an invaluable tool for promoting freedom, *real* freedom, and that a "drug magazine" would be impossible for the mainstream to buy out or co-opt. "Freedom of the press belongs to those who own one," Forcade noted in a 1976 editorial titled *"What High Times Is All About"* (see page 33). "We own one, and that's an important point. After all, it was the media that made marijuana illegal!"

From *High Times* to Cheech & Chong, marijuana culture flourished in the 1970s, bringing to full flower seeds nurtured in the '30s by jazz players, the '50s by beatniks, and the '60s by rock musicians. These artists defined the avant-garde of their respective eras while simultaneously serving as ambassadors for the herb, offering a positive, and public, example of pot smokers while most stoners stuck in the straight world rightfully feared for their safety. Coded references like Cab Calloway's song "Reefer Man" eventually gave way to overt admissions of marijiuana use from respected writers like Allen Ginsberg and Norman Mailer, who went on a nationally televised TV talk show in 1961 to advocate the spiritual and mind-expanding aspects of marijuana—the first honest discussion of the subject in the mainstream media. This was followed in the '70s by the free love and free weed vibe most closely associated with the Grateful Dead, a traveling carnival of freakdom whose legions of Deadhead followers provided an ideal distribution network for marijuana seeds, and increasingly sophisticated growing techniques, across the country.

Waldo 4:20 In 1971 in San Rafael, California, a group of students known among themselves as the Waldos began meeting every day at 4:20 P.M. to get

An early ad for the National Organization for the Reform of Marijuana Laws (NORML).

high under a statue of Louis Pasteur, eventually establishing their appointment for afternoon "high tea" as a slang term for the act of getting high itself. And so 4:20 was born, passed along informally on Grateful Dead tours for years and finally finding a home in *High Times'* monthly Pot 40 column. From there, the time-of-day connotation soon spread so far and wide that it eventually emerged as an entire day of celebration.

Each year on April 20 (4/20), stoners of all stripes share a high holiday, expressing their love for marijuana through art, activism, rallies, concerts, and a heck of a lot of getting stoned. Every culture has ceremonial days set aside for contemplation of the sacred, and with the advent of 4/20, marijuana smokers truly came of age. (Looking for a unique way to mark the occasion? Check out "420 Things to Do When You're Stoned," starting on page 104.)

The Modern Evolution of Cannabis Sativa   The plant itself also came of age in the '70s, a fertile time when Vietnam vets and wandering hippies returned to America, smuggling home exotic cannabis seeds from Thailand, Morocco, Colombia, Afghanistan, Nepal, and, of course, Vietnam and Cambodia. Amateur breeders on the West Coast quickly set natural selection loose in the drive to grow a better pot plant, crossbreeding the best of these genetic lines in informal experiments that ultimately yielded varieties that remain perennial favorites of growers and connoisseurs all over the world, including Northern Lights, White Widow, and Skunk #1.

As the War on Marijuana heated up, dealers started to depend less on imported crops, which had

Mellow Yellow, Amsterdam's first cannabis coffeeshop, opened for business in 1972.

to cross increasingly well-defended borders, and more on all-American weed, often grown indoors under high-intensity lights. In fact, breeders began to develop strains specifically engineered to thrive in these conditions, including hydroponic gardens that require no soil whatsoever.

These days, Amsterdam serves as the center of the cannabis universe, thanks to the Netherlands' tolerant stance on marijuana. In the 1960s, a group of young anarchistic Dutch students dubbed the Provos began "provoking" police, politicians, and other authorities through nonviolent guerrilla theater and public protest, demanding progressive changes in society, including an acceptance of marijuana. The Provos' focus on public education through outrageous "happenings" eventually inspired a larger, worldwide "hippie" movement. By 1972, Mellow Yellow, Amsterdam's first marijuana coffeeshop, had opened for business, and today, hundreds of coffeeshops operate in the

STONER SUBGENRES

Without a doubt, every pothead is unique. That's one of the beautiful things about marijuana culture—we resist stereotypes, no matter how hard society tries to pin us down. And yet, you do tend to find a lot more spliff smokers than usual at the concession stand of a reggae concert. So let's face facts: Certain ways of life have stoner written all over them, and at the risk of stereotyping ourselves, here's a quick guide to a few of the most prevalent pothead archetypes.

LEFTOVER HIPPIES Have you ever noticed that the old hippies who never stopped smoking weed tend to be the old hippies who never got lame? If you meet an old hippie in the road, smoke the old hippie out. If you are an old hippie in the road, keep on keeping on!

METALHEADS When you're nice and stoned, it's a lot easier to deal with one of those twenty-five-minute drum solos featuring crashing cymbals, satanic chants, and throwing up the horns the whole time.

POST PUNKS *This book's a bunch of shite and anyone who says they're punk rock totally isn't. And just cause I smoke pot don't make me a fucking stoner, and I sure as fuck don't need a fucking handbook to tell me how to get high, do I?*

HIP-HOPPERS More MCs name-check cannabis than Cristal and Cadillac combined. From Dre's *Chronic* to Cube's *Friday*, marijuana and the hip-hop lifestyle go together like blunts and raps.

HIPSTERS When you're nice and stoned, it's a lot easier to deal with one of those slow-moving foreign language films with characters that don't do anything except look out at desolate urban landscapes set to an avant-garde soundtrack.

SCI-FI AND COMIX GEEKS Every sci-fi/comix store in the world has either a secret basement storage room or an alley out back where the staff occasionally gathers to take hits out of a homemade Darth Vader helmet bong while arguing over who would grow better weed, Data from *Star Trek: The Next Generation* (hydro) or the Swamp Thing (organic outdoor).

SURFERS AND SKATERS Whether riding the ocean or the pavement, you've got to become one with both the board and the terrain, dude. Joel Tudor, the world's greatest longboard surfer, told *High Times* that smoking a joint before paddling out helps him find the one wave he's looking for from out of the vast blue sea, a skill that's essential not just in surfing, but also in life.

NEW AGERS

The Mayan calendar comes to an abrupt end on December 21, 2012, after 5,125 years of continuous cycles within cycles. If that doesn't blow your mind, try thinking it over after a joint, some yoga, and a little fire dancing. If *that* doesn't blow your mind, you're not going to like the New Age very much when it arrives.

PROFESSOR POTHEAD

Ever wish that college could last forever? Professor Pothead enjoyed getting stoned out on the quad and playing frisbee so much it turned into a lifelong career move. Seriously, scholarly types often like nothing better than rolling up a monster fattie, brewing some chamomile tea, and discussing the vagaries of existence. Kind of like college the first go 'round, except this time you're getting paid.

ANARCHO-ENVIRONMENTALISTS

After the coming ecological apocalypse rids us once and for all of the existing power structure, marijuana—or more likely hashish— will form the backbone of a new plant-based economy in tune with the Earth's ability to sustainably meet the needs of its populations. Imagine living in a brave new world with no oil, but plenty of good weed. Just remember to bring a lighter.

LIBERTARIANS

Freedom-loving libertarians will be damned if the government's going to come in and tell us stoners what to put in our bodies, for no good reason, never mind waste shitloads of our tax money doing it. Anyway, they don't often wear tie-dye, but lots of libertarian types puff weed, and their staunch political support is integral to the movement to legalize marijuana.

AVERAGE JOES (AND JANES)

Nothing beats coming home from a tough day at work, having a nice dinner, taking care of chores, and then curling up in bed with a fat joint and a rerun of *The Simpsons*. In fact, let's go nuts and throw a little low-fat ice milk into the equation. Make it a party.

It takes all kinds of potheads to make the world go 'round . . . even a few who still feel the need to camouflage their love of cannabis.

Netherlands, legally selling weed, hash, and pot foods, while countless small storefronts sell marijuana seeds both over the counter and through the mail. In 1988, *High Times* hosted the first Cannabis Cup, now an annual international competition that pits Amsterdam's coffeeshops and seed breeders from all over the world against each other in a contest to crown the best weed on Earth. (Want to know "How to Survive the Cannabis Cup"? Well, you could certainly be forgiven for skipping ahead to page 48.)

Everybody's Doing It In 1976, former peanut farmer Jimmy Carter took office with a young, ambitious, and highly progressive administration that sought the all-out decriminalization of marijuana, and planned to build upon a movement for reform that was already making gains.

President Carter's son, Chip, partied with NORML founder Keith Stroup, whose team also played softball against the administration's staff. Things hit their high point when none other than Willie Nelson was invited to perform at the White House and also sleep over. In the middle of the night, the Red Headed Stranger got out of bed, snuck onto the roof, and lit up a joint. (Could he have imagined that thirty years later, he'd still be getting busted for weed, most recently in 2006, when a pound and a half of grass and more than three ounces of magic mushrooms were seized on his tour bus?)

"Marijuana is like sex," Nelson wrote in his 1988 biography *Willie*, by way of explaining his White House escapade. "If I don't do it every day, I get a headache."

By 1978, however, the party was over. Peter Bourne, Carter's presidential point man on drug issues, resigned his position after admitting to writing a fraudulent prescription for sedatives for a coworker and getting high at a NORML-sponsored party. Plans to decriminalize marijuana were scuttled, and the reform movement wouldn't regain its momentum for decades. Still, the hip culture's easy acceptance of pot as "no big deal" in the '70s, rather than as a signal of radical beliefs, as in the '60s, increasingly moved marijuana into the mainstream. All but the most square quickly accepted the then barely illegal drug, whether they experimented or not, as part of a postwar hedonism that also made popular entertainment of streaking, wife-swapping, psychotherapy, self-help books, and disco.

This arrival in the mainstream unfortunately had the equal and opposite reaction of outraging certain elements of society sufficiently to start their own organized opposition to any loosening of the marijuana laws. Although compelling evidence points to cannabis's use as a sacrament by early Jewish and Christian worshipers (see "Holy Smokes" page 37), those practices have since been suppressed. In fact, right-wing religious organizations played a key role in the rise of "concerned parents groups," which started forming in the late '70s and went on to serve as foot soldiers in Ronald Reagan's devastating campaign to relaunch the War on Drugs in the 1980s. And so we got "Just Say No!" "What About the Children?" D.A.R.E. (Drug Abuse Resistance Education), cops telling lies in school, expensive pot, cheap cocaine,

Scarface, a lot of wasted money, and too many wasted lives.

Footnote: When the B-movie-actor turned President "Raygun" behind all this bullshit was caught red-handed selling weapons to Islamic fundamentalists in Iran (our sworn enemies) in order to help fund an illegal armed insurrection by right-wing cocaine-trafficking Contras in Nicaragua (whose illicit exports went almost exclusively to the United States), nobody seemed to get too upset, because the Drug War is all about ideology, not reality. *Drugs are bad, m'kay?*—period.

For example, on September 5, 1989, the first President George Bush held up a bag of crack for the cameras during a speech broadcast live to the nation, claiming the rocks had been "seized a few days ago in a park across the street from the White House." True enough. But the president failed to mention that the DEA lured the poor kid they busted all the way from southeast D.C. to Lafayette Park, solely for the purposes of dramatic oratory. Nor did Bush mention the dealer's response (*"Where the fuck is the White House?"*) when the narcs first suggested the location.

Less than a month after his "crack speech," Bush the First launched his DEA-executed Operation Green Merchant, a coordinated raid on hydroponic stores in forty-six states (including some of *High Times'* biggest advertisers). While crack spread havoc in the ghetto, the Feds focused on keeping gardening products off the shelf. No longer content to hassle smokers, smugglers, dealers, and growers, the government now had its sights set on businesses supplying perfectly legal

products, lest the marijuana-industrial complex grow large enough to one day lobby for its rights.

And no, things didn't get much better under Bill Clinton. The Non-Inhaler-in-Chief may have been the first president to come of age in the '60s, but for pot smokers, his two terms in office were a far cry from the Age of Aquarius. Clinton fought against California's Prop 215 in 1996, which approved medical marijuana for the first time, and then backed raids on medical marijuana gardens and dispensaries after it passed. He also oversaw the arrest of five million marijuana smokers during his eight years in power, setting a record surpassed only by his less-than-illustrious successor.

As for George W. Bush, instinct alone should tell you how much worse it's gotten under his administration. Despite living in a post-9/11 world, Bush's drug warriors have found the time, manpower, and resources to target paraphernalia sellers

Hunter S. Thompson salutes NORML founder Keith Stroup.

with massive federal sting operations, arrest more pot smokers than any previous administration, and, perhaps most heinous of all, pay for Super Bowl advertisements comparing America's five million regular marijuana smokers to Al Qaeda terrorists. Frankly, we expected better from the first president to admit to inhaling (although he probably calls it "inhalating").

"I wouldn't answer the marijuana question," Bush boasted during his first run for the Oval Office in a private conversation secretly audiotaped by longtime friend Doug Wead (some friend; nice name). "I don't want any kid doing what I tried to do thirty years ago. . . . Do you want your little kid to say, 'Hey, Daddy, President Bush tried marijuana—I think I will?'" Basically, Bush believes it's perfectly fine to elect a pot-smoking, lying hypocrite, as long as it's him.

☘ WEED SHALL OVERCOME

But don't let these bastards take away your pride or your optimism. We've got the plant and the truth on our side, and sooner rather than later we're going to prevail. Their failed War on Marijuana depends on ideology, so we must develop a *high*deology for counterbalance—a philosophy and strategy dedicated to declaring peace and ending the insanity once and for all.

Yes, it's always important to say what pot smokers *aren't*: violent, criminal, addicted, stupid, spaced-out, dopey, unmotivated, etc. But it's also high time we take the next step forward, and start talking about what pot smokers *are*: kind, for one thing. Tolerant, for another.

Hopefully, this humble little handbook will help you feel proud to be part of a culture that's older than history, and yet still waiting to be fully free. Remember (at least in the *long* term): Every time two heads get together to burn one down, the cannabis continuum adds another page to the Big Book of Buddha—never mind that we may one day rip it out to roll a joint.

FREE-MARKET MARIJUANA

Milton Friedman and 500 other economists in support of legal pot

"There is no logical basis for the prohibition of marijuana," according to Nobel Prize–winning economist Milton Friedman (*fried, man*), a leading voice in the promotion of free-market economics, a founding father of the Reagan Revolution, and about as far from a "hippie" as you're likely to find on planet Earth. As Friedman declared shortly before his death at age 94: "It's absolutely disgraceful to think of picking up a 22-year-old for smoking pot. More disgraceful is the denial of marijuana for medical purposes."

As you might imagine, Mr. Friedman had money on his mind as well as marijuana—$13.9 billion to be exact, the total the United States would stand to gain each year by replacing prohibition with a system of taxation and regulation similar to alcohol, according to a 2005 report prepared by Jeffrey A. Miron—a visiting professor of economics at Harvard University—and endorsed by Friedman and over five hundred other economists from around the country. The overall figure represents $7.7 billion saved annually in state and federal expenditures on prohibition enforcement, plus an additional $6.2 billion in tax revenue generated by legal marijuana sales.

The report, whimsically titled "Budgetary Implications of Marijuana Prohibition in the United States," can be read in its entirety at www.prohibitioncosts.org.

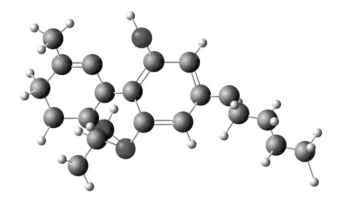

Of the seventy known herbal cannabinoids, tetrahydrocannabinol (THC), cannabidiol (CBD), and cannabinol (CBN) are the most prevalent, and their medical properties have received the most study.

TETRAHYDROCANNABINOL (THC)

Better known as THC, tetrahydrocannabinol is the most famous of marijuana's active ingredients, though hardly the only compound in cannabis that gets you stoned. A complex interplay of over seventy known cannabinoids accounts for the plant's *highly* unique effect on the brain.

THC was first isolated in 1964 by a team led by Israeli researcher Raphael Mechoulam, who recently admitted to *High Times* that he's still "experimenting" with cannabis-based medicines, most recently as a cure for post-traumatic stress disorder. "When I started to work on cannabis in 1963, I thought the project would take me a couple of months, but forty years later, we're still working," he explained. "We discovered cannabis is part of a very, very basic system of the brain that was unknown at that time—it became known later because of this work."

Follow-up research also confirmed the existence of specific receptors in the brain for cannabinoids, including THC, which means that the body naturally produces substances similar to those found in marijuana as part of normal brain function. This explains a lot about the plant's amazing medical properties and low toxicity.

In 1986, the FDA approved synthetic THC, known by the trade name Marinol, for use as a prescription drug. Created entirely within the laboratory, without any pesky pot plants, and therefore a source of potential profits for the pharmaceutical industry, Marinol was quickly endorsed by politicians as the answer to medical marijuana, despite the fact that a pill with one synthetic ingredient failed to replicate the complex reactions that occur when ingesting real buds. Nevertheless, any attempted research into the medical benefits of marijuana was effectively blocked for decades

Meanwhile, most patients rated natural marijuana as far superior to synthetic THC, and so the medical marijuana movement has rolled on. Today,

GW Pharmaceuticals has approval in Canada to sell Sativex (see "Just Spray No" page 160), a whole-plant extract of cannabis that includes not only all-natural THC, but all of the other cannabinoids present in pot.

HEAD STONER IN CHARGE

High Times *founder Tom Forcade*

All but lost to highstory, *High Times* founder Tom Forcade led a brief, troubled, but ultimately triumphant life, often underground and always full speed ahead. At once a marijuana smuggler, weed dealer, renegade publisher, political activist, cosmic prankster, and early adherent to the punk

High Times *founder Tom Forcade, dressed as alter-ego "Reverend Tom," reads a prepared statement prior to throwing a pie in the face of Professor Otto N. Larsen during the President's Commission on Obscenity and Pornography hearings in Washington, D.C., in 1970.*

movement and its sense of anarchy, Forcade came of age hot-rodding in his native Arizona, often having occasion to outrace the local police in the famed Bonneville Salt Flats. From his high-octane teenage years until his death in 1978 at age 33, the young outlaw from the wild West always felt most comfortable one step ahead of the law.

Not just bold, Tom Forcade was also brilliant, graduating from the University of Utah's business administration program in just two and a half years. Given his antiestablishment leanings, the choice of such a seemingly square college major reveals Forcade's approach to revolution as a serious endeavor, requiring commitment, strategy, and plenty of money. But whether he was flying in a multiton shipment of Santa Marta Gold from Colombia or launching a national magazine in praise of America's last taboo pleasure, the profit potential of each mission was always secondary to the thrill of adventure and the opportunity to support his favorite causes. Along with leaving $10,000 in cash on the doorstep of the National Organization for the Reform of Marijuana Laws (NORML) with an anonymous note encouraging other marijuana dealers to do the same, he also helped form the Rock Liberation Front to shake down major rock music promoters and make them donate a portion of their profits back to the emerging youth culture that had made them rich in the first place.

Like Robin Hood before him, Forcade broke the law with honor.

It all started in the early '60s, with a fateful trip across the country in a psychedelic school bus, a journey that ended in New York City, which would become Forcade's adopted hometown. Arriving in a freewheeling, swashbuckling era with mild pot laws and relatively little enforcement, Forcade smuggled marijuana into America as part of a loose-knit, anarchistic brotherhood known as the Hippie Mafia.

Far-wandering flower children had found insanely cheap high-grade herb all over the world, and returning Vietnam vets knew how to pilot small planes, navigate international waters, and organize the military-style operations necessary to bring it back home to America. For his part, Forcade flew down to South America, rode ferry boats out to meet supply ships, drove getaway cars faster than the cops could follow, and once, when he couldn't escape on wings, water, or wheels, took off on foot, subsequently spending two days stuck in the middle of a swamp, soaking wet and surrounded, until he finally crawled past the police barricade inch by inch on his hands and knees while the pigs sat in their cars to avoid the mosquitoes.

With pot coming in by the planeload, offloaded by forklift, and secured in stash houses set up all over New York City, Forcade oversaw a vast and profitable empire and used his clout, connections, and free-flowing cannabis to establish himself as a major player in the radical politics of the time, albeit usually behind the scenes. Despite his business degree, this was one "hip" capitalist who never saw his illicit operations as a way to get rich or famous, but rather as a revenue stream capable of funding his higher callings.

In 1967, long before starting *High Times*, Forcade founded the Underground Press Syndicate (UPS),

which collected the best content from the hundreds of alternative newspapers sprouting up across the country during the psychedelic '60s, and made this content available for reprint in other publications and on microfiche in university libraries. In 1970, Forcade edited Yippie cofounder Abbie Hoffman's *Steal This Book*, a collaboration that yielded a brilliant field guide to fomenting social revolution, but also a feud that would mark Forcade's break with the established antiestablishmentarianists. He would go on to form the Zippies, in opposition to both the Vietnam War and his one-time Yippie cohorts, claiming his former comrades had gone soft in the fight against imperialist America.

When the Zippies decided to crash the 1972 Republican National Convention, the result was an indictment for Forcade for planning to firebomb the event—trumped-up charges later dropped by the FBI for lack of evidence. Meanwhile, the

Tom Forcade shares a podium with novelist Gore Vidal and Yippie cohorts Abbie Hoffman and Jerry Rubin.

UPS disintegrated after pressure from the CIA led the major record labels to stop advertising in the underground press. As a result, the number of alternative magazines dropped precipitously.

Forcade felt the repression coming, and tried to warn his fellow editors at the 1969 Revolutionary Media Conference in Ann Arbor: "The United Press Syndicate papers, as advance scouts for journalism in Amerika and the world, often find themselves in conflict with uptight Smokey-the-Bears of the totalitarian forest, rushing around with paralegal shovels and axe-wielding blue meanie henchmen, stomping out the fires of a people who have found their voice and are using it . . . ," Forcade told his colleagues. "You're going to have to identify some sort of base that the straight press can't co-opt. Either sex, drugs, or politics."

Always a savvy entrepreneur, Forcade understood that to truly succeed in publishing he needed an idea the corporations couldn't co-opt and a group of advertisers the straight world couldn't scare off. Still heavily involved in the lucrative marijuana trade, he dropped $20,000 of his own money into a new venture: *High Times* magazine. Hoping to do for drugs what Hugh Hefner's *Playboy* had done for sex, Forcade's timing couldn't have been better. In 1974, when the first issue premiered, countless Americans were discovering the joys of marijuana as the hippie sacrament became increasingly ingrained in mainstream culture. Meanwhile, just a year earlier, the DEA had formed in response to Richard Nixon's call for an all-out War on Drugs.

The stakes in this new war were high, but fortunately, so was Forcade, his magazine, and its readers. The earliest issues of *High Times* served the interests of smokers, smugglers, and growers alike, offering such sought-after but hard-to-find information as how to make hash oil, where to plant outdoors, and which airplanes work best for concealing a few tons of weed.

An immediate, smashing success, *High Times* would double its readership every issue for years, quickly reaching millions of potheads each month, while making its anonymous publisher rich and influential almost overnight. Still, dark days loomed ahead for our hero. Suffering from the manic depression that had stalked him since his father's death when he was 11, Forcade became increasingly paranoid and erratic, although perhaps an herb-smuggling, weed-dealing, drug-magazine-publishing revolutionary can never be too careful.

Always a loner, Forcade restricted his inner circle to himself and his trusted associate and friend, Jack Coombs. Increasingly in conflict with friends, lovers, and his own magazine, the boss would arrive in the office in a drug-fueled rage, fire everyone in sight, rip the phones from the wall, and then apologize the next day and restore order. One night he'd be up till dawn reviewing the current issue and planning new stories; the next day he'd talk about shutting down operations.

When times got toughest, Forcade would drop back into the underground and resume his smuggling operations. Most at ease in situations the rest of us would find unbearable, he found sweet relief in living on the edge, but when a botched mission led to a plane crash over the Everglades and the death of his best friend, he never really recovered.

Bringing in a shipment of herb from Colombia in the spring of 1978, Forcade, in the lead plane, kept instructing his pilot to fly lower, just above the treetops, to avoid detection. They made it across, but the plane behind them dipped too low and went down in a ball of flames.

All throughout the following summer, Forcade stayed in denial, convinced that his buddy Coombs had miraculously survived the crash, even hiring private investigators to search for him. Suddenly without his best friend, confidant, and coconspirator when he needed him most, Forcade became increasingly withdrawn and depressed as the winter approached. In November, just four years after founding the magazine that would carry on his legacy, he committed suicide, and the hip world lost one of its brightest shining stars.

Wholly unaware of the passing of this legendary underground outlaw, the *New York Times* published no obituary for Tom Forcade, but his 1976 mission statement, "What *High Times* Is All About," serves as a clear declaration of his hopes and dreams for the magazine, as well as an inspiring eulogy for the uncompromising man who made it all happen.

WHAT *HIGH TIMES* IS ALL ABOUT *by Thomas King Forcade*

The general public (us) has no idea who really owns and manages *Time* magazine, the *Washington Post*, the *New York Times*, the three monopolistic TV networks, Random House, Simon & Schuster, and so on.

Nor do we have any idea what their goals are.

And the public will never learn from the aforementioned sources, either. Many fine people work for the straight media, but as A. J. Liebling said, freedom of the press belongs to those who own one. We own one, and that's an important point. After all, it was the media that made marijuana illegal! Their pot scare campaigns created the temporary popular support that made it politically expedient to outlaw marijuana. The media (except for the underground press) fully cooperated in getting us and keeping us in the Vietnam War, and, after ten years of mass demonstrations, the media finally helped get us out. The media put Nixon in (over 90 percent of the daily newspapers endorsed his candidacy in 1972, Watergate notwithstanding), and the media finally got rid of Nixon just a year later by publishing the truth. So you have a right to know.

Trans High Corporation (THC—the parent company of *High Times*) was started to bring new consciousness projects into reality, particularly projects within the media. As we stated some time ago, we have no particular interest in manufacturing rolling papers or hash pipes, or starting *High Times* key clubs. We are mainly interested in opening up communication, providing access to information. One of the first THC projects was *High Times* magazine. It was a coldly conceived project, there was nothing accidental about it, and we definitely expected it to succeed, eventually. Instead, it took off like a rocket, right from the beginning, and

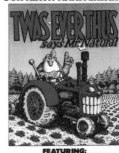

From the looks of it, Dan would rather sit next to someone else.

our main problem has been holding on. Holding on—to our personal identities, to our editorial independence, to our corporate independence, to reality, to our rapport and unique communication with our readers, to our sanity. Coping with the staggering business-financial-organizational problems caused by our rapid growth. Finding honest, competent, creative people to be the staff. And retaining our perspective amidst a barrage of publicity—all of it strangely favorable.

To outsiders, the *High Times* "success story" appears to be a typical capitalist trip, with one or more individuals on top raking in tons of money to be used for buying Lamborghini sports cars, MacIntosh stereos, penthouses, Peruvian flake, and sexual companionship that resembles the people in the cigarette ads as closely as possible. While we assure you that we at *High Times*

fully appreciate the value of hedonism (learned in part from that pioneering personal researcher in the field, Hugh M. Hefner), the fact is that THC is owned by a nonprofit trust fund and the staff makes very modest salaries indeed. Should we make any excess profits, they will be given to organizations concerned with social, political, and economic change. We'd like to own MacIntosh stereos, but other things are more important to us. Like putting out the best magazine imaginable. A magazine that has always been far more than a "dope" magazine. Lately, as you have seen, we have been broadening our scope even more. It is obvious that our readers want to hear about a broad range of contemporary and historical subjects. We have no desire to be limited to being the magazine of substances that people put in their mouths. In this issue, you will notice more general news, more diverse features, much more music coverage, and more cultural and political coverage than ever before. We have continued and expanded our policy of using name authors and experts from every field, including top-notch investigative reporters, fiction writers, new journalists, old journalists, better editing, and hard-core dopers who know what they're talking about (we've been there too, folks). Meanwhile, we will continue to have the best, the most accurate, the most interesting and entertaining, the most wide-ranging, creative, wild, courageous coverage of dope anywhere. If you see any serious competition, let us know.

Making money is not enough for us. Money and political "power" (often a goal in publishing) strike us as irrelevant. We are faced with a future that needs help. We know that as far as the future is concerned, we are playing for keeps. Our goal is to go all the way, whatever that may bring.

HOLY SMOKES
Was Jesus a stoner?

He had long hair and a shaggy beard. He shunned the working life and advocated dropping out of the capitalist economy. He pissed off the establishment by traveling the countryside preaching a gospel of peace, love, and brotherhood to an ever-growing following of dedicated dreamers. No, not Jerry Garcia—we're talking about Jesus Christ.

Known in ancient Hebrew as the "anointed one," Jesus not only submitted to his own immersion in holy anointing oil, he passed the practice along to his apostles, instructing them to take the "blessing" around the world.

"And they cast out many devils, and anointed with oil many that were sick, and healed them" (Mark 6:13). Oh, by the way, the anointing oil recipe in the Old Testament [Exodus 30:22–23] included over six pounds of *kaneh-bosem*, better known as cannabis flowers, extracted into about six quarts of olive oil—more than enough herb to induce a powerfully psychedelic experience when absorbed through the skin.

Not that J. C. was the first, or last, advocate for medical marijuana. Thousands of years before Jesus was born, the healing powers of pot were already well known in China, and the plant has since been scientifically proven effective in the treatment of many ailments cured by Jesus and his early Christian apostles.

AMERICA'S #1 CASH CROP

Despite intensive eradication efforts, America's pot production has increased more than tenfold since 1981, with California, Tennessee, Kentucky, Hawaii, and Washington leading the way. So just how much is the entire U.S. harvest of homegrown marijuana worth in the marketplace? Using conservative estimates, around $35 billion per year—more than corn and wheat combined—making the devil's lettuce the nation's #1 cash crop.

For a mere 35 billion dollars, you can buy all the pot in America. Just make sure you remember to share, okay?

Chapter 2

SKILLS

You may not think it takes a lot of skill to smoke pot, and perhaps you're right, but keep this in mind before you decide: Bill Clinton was a Rhodes scholar in 1968, when he spent a year studying abroad at Oxford, Great Britain's oldest and most prestigious institute of higher learning, and yet despite all of this fancy education, the saxophone-playing college kid who would one day grow up to be president of the United States apparently had no idea how to properly react when a fellow "Oxford Man" passed him a joint.

"When I was in England, I experimented with marijuana a time or two, and I didn't like it. I didn't inhale and never tried it again," Clinton told reporters during his first run for the nation's highest office, setting off not only a few snickers at his less than forthright response, but also a loud fit of coughing from the stoners in the back of the room who felt he might have enjoyed the experience a bit more if he'd actually, you know, *inhaled*. After all, if you're going to "experiment," you really should allow an opportunity for the active ingredient to take effect before drawing any conclusions.

Anyway, for the purposes of this handbook, we're going to go ahead and assume you've already mastered the fine art of toking on a joint, pipe, blunt, bowl, or bong, and that you're now ready to move on to some of the higher-level functions you'll need to master in order to transform yourself into a truly skilled stoner. Remember, a well-rolled spliff says a lot more than just *let's go burn one*—it also shows that you've devoted the time and effort it takes to do things right when it comes to getting high.

Dedicated marijuana smokers don't have a secret handshake, but we do have a few ways to distinguish ourselves from the masses, including an elaborate set of slang words and some not-so-strict rules of etiquette all our own. So kindly understand that if you roll up a loose, wrinkly joint and take *three* hits before you pass it in the wrong direction, everyone in the circle will suddenly realize that it's amateur hour.

Just as the jocks always know who won the big game and the sci-fi geeks know the difference between *Voyager* and *Deep Space Nine*, if you really enjoy cannabis, you should be up for learning all you can about this most beneficent of plants and the underground culture that loves it. Like most of the finer things in life, you'll find that marijuana becomes infinitely more pleasurable the more you understand the proper ways to share and enjoy it.

HEADIQUETTE

Minding your marijuana manners may sound like a joke, but it's no laughing matter when some clown joins your circle and sucks down half the joint before it gets around once, or, even worse, offers to "chip in a couple dollars" if only you'll roll another one. Remember, when somebody smokes you up, friend or stranger, they're sharing something both illegal and expensive, not to mention medicinal and spiritual, so treat them and the offering with respect. It also never hurts to say thank you. And, naturally, remember to return the favor the next time circumstances allow. For karma's sake, if nothing else.

Basically, most headiquette boils down to respecting both the herb and your fellow herbalists. Don't talk about weed in public and don't light up unless everyone you're with feels comfortable. Don't show up just before a session and leave right after, unless that's the plan. Don't get the munchies and eat all your cousin's leftover macaroni and cheese, unless she's cool with it.

Then there's the little stuff that only a stoner would know. Like never handing over a bowl that might be cashed without fair warning. Or never ashing in a clean bong. Or never asking someone where they get their grass until you know them well. And, of course, never, ever knocking on the door and pretending to be the cops.

Most potheads are pretty forgiving (except for the cop thing), so mind your manners, but don't sweat the small stuff and don't be afraid to ask questions. For example, the three etiquette inquiries *High Times* receives most frequently:

1. IS IT OKAY TO MAKE A PROFIT WHEN SELLING WEED TO YOUR FRIENDS?

If it's a regular thing, a reasonable fee for your time, trouble, and risk is more than fair. If it's a one-time "solid" for a good buddy, then no, it's not cool.

2. I ACCIDENTALLY BROKE MY SISTER'S BONG. DO I HAVE TO REPLACE IT?

Tough one. Bongs break—it's a sad fact of life. If you've got the scratch to spare, you might offer to split the cost of a new one, but if replacing the bong creates a hardship, well, your sister will have to understand that it was an accident and absorb the loss. Perhaps you've got a cherished piece of paraphernalia you can offer up in the name of cosmic rebalancing.

3. CAN YOU GUYS HOOK ME UP WITH SOME BUDS?

We're a magazine, okay?—not a delivery service. And it's sort of rude of you to put us on the spot like that. Yes, weed can sometimes be a little hard to locate, but dude, you need to be a bit more dis-creet when it comes to supplying your demand.

JOINT SESSION

There's an old joke about a man holding a violin case who flags down a taxi in Times Square and asks the driver if he knows how to get to Carnegie Hall. "Practice, practice, practice," replies the cabbie, and the maxim holds true whether you want to play first chair in a symphony orchestra or simply produce pitch-perfect joints. You've got to practice, so go get a pack of papers and a sack of weed, sit down somewhere pleasant, and just start rolling one after another until you get it right. Sooner than you think, you'll enter a secret society with millions of members and only one rule: You've got to roll your own way.

Travel the world or attend a single Allman Brothers concert, and you'll find ample evidence that no two stoners approach rolling joints with exactly the same method. In fact, you can tell a lot about a pothead by the way they twist one up. Fat blunts or toothpick-sized pinners? Smooth and elegant cigarettes or wrinkled doobies that

Two girls gone ganja share one perfectly rolled joint.

HOW TO RO

A Spliff

TOP: *Use your two lips to smoke this tulip shaped spliff*
ABOVE: *Roll, roll, roll your bone . . .*

get bumpy in the middle? Filters or cones? Spliffs or six papers stuck together to make one monster cannon that holds a quarter ounce? No matter how *you* decide to roll, it's essential to find and develop your own unique style.

But style, as always, remains secondary to function. First, you've got to get to the point where if you get stuck on a desert island with weed, papers, and a lighter, you'll soon be getting high. Only then will you become a truly self-reliant stoner, and everything after that is just showing off—not that showing off is always such a bad thing. In the meantime, here's a few tips for beginners on the basics of the art form.

1. Always "clean" your weed before rolling, removing all stems and seeds.

2. Use a hand grinder or scissors on buds, stopping before they get powdery.

3. Use high-quality rolling papers. Put a fold in the middle and fill the fold with ground-up herb. Roll the paper back and forth over the buds until they form a compacted tube at the bottom of the fold. You may need to rearrange some of the marijuana before a tight tube will form.

4. Fold the half of the rolling paper *without* glue as tightly as possible around the tube of weed and then roll the whole thing up to the top with your thumbs. Stop when you reach the glue.

5. Lick the glue thoroughly, but don't soak it. Continue rolling until the glue sticks. You may need to use a small stick or a stem to push the buds in from the sides before sparking it up.

DEALING WITH YOUR DEALER

Your dealer might be your best friend or some guy you meet in a mall parking lot once every two weeks. A balding hippie with a gray ponytail, a hip-hop head in a hoodie, or a young skater chick with cool tattoos. It takes all kinds, so to speak. Some dealers sell a little on the side so they can smoke for free, and some find themselves heavily involved in a full-time hustle. Whatever the nature of your relationship with your reefer man (or reefer woman), there are still ten solid commandments to keep in mind when it comes to dealing with your dealer:

1. THOU SHALT NOT HAGGLE *Marijuana is definitely a take it or leave it proposition.*

2. THOU SHALT NOT DAWDLE *If your dealer wants you to stick around and get high, you'll be invited; otherwise do your business and move along.*

3. THOU SHALT NOT BRING A FRIEND WITHOUT PERMISSION, FOR OBVIOUS REASONS

4. THOU SHALT NOT ASK FOR A FREE SAMPLE

5. THOU SHALT NOT ASK TO BE FRONTED WEED UNTIL NEXT TUESDAY

6. THOU SHALT NOT ASK WHERE THINE DEALER GETS HERB FROM OR HOW MUCH IT COSTS

7. THOU SHALT NOT TALK ABOUT HERB ON THE PHONE OR EMAIL

8. THOU SHALT NOT MAKE A SCENE *This means no loud music booming out of your car windows on the way in or hysterical laughter on the way out.*

9. THOU SHALT NOT EXPECT YOUR DEALER TO SMOKE YOU OUT ALL THE TIME AND NEVER RETURN THE FAVOR *After all, didn't you just get a brand-new fat sack of weed?*

10. THOU SHALT NOT BUG THE SHIT OUT OF YOUR DEALER DURING THE OCCASIONAL DRY SPELL

FILTER TIPS

Once you've got your joints down pat, move on to adding a filter by placing a small tube of cardboard at one end of the rolling paper before you add the weed and roll it up. This will make your joint a little smoother and also let you burn it down to the end without having to deal with hot fingers, roach clips, or ash in your mouth.

GENERATION JOINTS

Not every joint gets finished. What's left behind is universally known as a *roach*, presumably because of its resemblance to a cockroach. Usually there's not much worth saving, but sometimes a decent-sized roach finds it way onto the coffee table. Peel back the singed paper and you'll find a choice little nugget of bud in there, nicely cured by the smoke that's already passed through it on the way to your mouth.

Collect seven sizable roaches and roll them together. That's a *first-generation joint*, strong and smooth. Roll up the roaches from seven first-generation joints, and you're puffing a *second-generation joint*, a dankly decadent smoke requiring the harvest of fifty roaches. To reach the seventh generation, you'd have to roll 823,543 joints. If you start today and smoke three joints per day, saving every roach, it will only take 754 years to achieve this worthy goal.

Better get rolling.

AS AMERICAN AS APPLE PIPE

Less than two weeks after 9/11, dozens of federal agents were deployed on a raid in Sarasota, Florida. The target was not a suspected Al Qaeda sleeper cell, as you might imagine, but the home and offices of Chris Hill, owner of CHILLS Tobacco, a purveyor of fine "smoking accessories" with over $3 million in annual sales. In 2003, the Bush administration again found the time and money to protect America from bongs, launching Operation Pipe Dreams and Operation Headhunter, which put fifty-five people out of business, and put Tommy Chong behind bars for nine months.

Freedom-loving stoners have to ask themselves: Just how far are the Feds willing to take the misguided metaphor that is the War on Drugs? How will we smoke if they take every bong, bowl, chillum, pipe, and paper away from us? Okay, that will never happen, but it's still comforting to know that if you ever break your three-foot, double-chamber, dragon-shaped glass pipe, you can always use a Bic pen and an apple to craft a fully functional replacement.

Smoke from the forbidden fruit when you're on the road, at the beach, visiting Grandma, or anywhere else you don't have access to your usual arsenal of pot paraphernalia. In fact, why stop with just one edible implement, when you can smoke an apple pipe for knowledge, a carrot to treat cataracts, and a potato for St. Patrick's Day? And when you're done, simply take a bite out of crime, and swallow the evidence.

🍃 HOW TO MAKE AN APPLE PIPE

1. Remove the ink tube from a disposable pen so you have its hollow plastic holder with nothing inside.

2. Jam the pen halfway into the apple at a shallow angle. Start near the core where it's easiest to push it in. This will eventually be your bowl.

3. On the opposite side of the apple, poke another hole that meets up with the first. This is where your lips will go.

4. Poke another connecting hole closer to the bowl, which will serve as a carb. Keep your finger over the carb when you light the bowl and then release your finger to clear the smoke in the pipe.

5. Use a knife to carve out the bowl deep enough to hold at least one solid hit's worth of weed, and start smoking!

THE G-SPOT

Gravity bongs pack a wallop, harnessing one of nature's most powerful forces and using it to produce milky-white bong rips that shouldn't be taken lightly, even by the most seasoned of smokers. One second you're asking how it works, or better yet *explaining* how it works, and the next you're glued to the couch, trying to remember your aunt's first name . . . it's right there on the tip of your tongue. . . . And then you look up and two hours have passed. It's *that* kind of stoned.

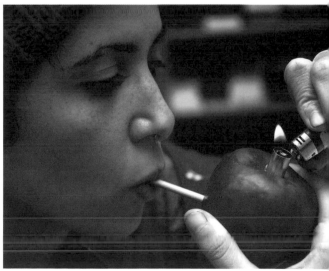

An apple pipe per day chases the blues away.

As the name implies, this simple device creates a vacuum and then uses gravity to fill it with billowy pot smoke, saving your lungs the trouble of clouding up the container and also creating the distinct possibility that you will bite off more than you can chew. Still, this cough-inducing dorm room classic is easy to construct, costs next to nothing, and makes a perfect project for a rainy day. Use only as directed.

GRAVITY BONG

1 two-liter bottle

1 "bowl piece" from a bong

1 bucket of water, deep enough to submerge the bottle

1. Using a sharp knife, remove the bottom section from a 2-liter bottle.

2. Heat the point of the knife with a lighter, then punch a small hole through the bottle's plastic cap. Carefully push the stem of your bowl piece through the hole, melting the cap as necessary to widen the hole, and/or using chewing gum to make an airtight seal.

3. Submerge the bottle without affixing the cap, leaving enough room above the surface to grip the top of the bottle. Loosely pack some herb in the bowl and screw the top on firmly, then slowly raise the bottle out of the water while lighting the bowl.

4. Unscrew the bottle cap carefully, then slowly resubmerge the bottle while ingesting the smoke.

HOW TO SURVIVE THE CANNABIS CUP *A heavy-user's guide to the world's greatest pot party*

They arrive in Amsterdam like the huddled masses of immigrants who landed on Ellis Island at the end of the 19th century: tired, cold, dazed, confused, and yearning—in this case, *yearning to be stoned*. These pothead pilgrims reach the Cannabis Cup registration center in groups of two, three, sometimes ten or more, often fresh from the airport, all seeking a new life in the land of marijuana freedom, if only for the next five days. They're handed one of over two thousand numbered, laminated judges' badges, and instantly join an electorate representing a broad cross-section of humanity, assembled from every corner of the globe: the young and the old; black, white, and all shades in between; Christians, Jews, Muslims, Buddhists, Rastafarians, Satanists, agnostics, atheists, and those who just pray to God that someday pot will be legal both where they live and around the world. All of them brought together by the simple love of a sacred plant, and to take part in what Cannabis Cup founder Steven Hager calls, with palpable understatement, a "harvest festival."

For more than twenty years, the Cannabis Cup has been the world's premier marijuana event, bringing together aficionados from around the world to crown the best cannabis from Amsterdam's famous "coffeeshops." Judges can expect to choose from over twenty strains of marijuana, plus a plethora of hash, and since finding enough time to smoke it all can present a real high-class problem, here are a few tips to make sure you're still standing when the smoke clears.

⚜ DRINK WATER

You should be thirsty for adventure in Amsterdam, not water. Cottonmouth can run rampant at the Cannabis Cup, and dehydration does far worse than just impair cognition; it also totally kills your buzz. You will hear all about "meltdowns" at the Cup—poor, lost souls who went five tokes over the line—but "meltdown," with its implication of abundant water, is often an ironic misnomer. Most "Amsterdamage" actually occurs when people don't drink enough *agua*.

High Times recommends roughly one glass of water per joint for optimal performance. Your results may vary.

⚜ SMOKE WITH YOUR HEAD, NOT OVER IT

A dutiful judge at the Cannabis Cup must sample a new strain every four hours (more or less, if you plan to sleep). It's a challenge and a joy any way you roll it, but if you remember to pace yourself, you'll enjoy it all the more.

One of the great things separating pot smokers from alcohol drinkers is that, generally speaking, we don't go on and on about how much we inhaled last night, as opposed to the bravado with which boozers often describe their latest alcoholic debauchery. Amsterdam, however, tends to be the exception to this reefer rule. Finally allowed out into polite society, we stoners forget how to behave

TOP: *DNA Genetics' Cannabis Cup entry proves that good breeding still counts for something.*
ABOVE: *Every November, the* High Times *Cannabis Cup in Amsterdam awards the most coveted prizes in pot.*

HOW TO ORDER OFF A COFFEESHOP MENU

Indicas, sativas, *hashish, and ganja-infused foods—what's a simple stoner to do?*

The first time you walk into a coffeeshop in Amsterdam, you'll think to yourself: *Holy shit, it's real! Even seeing it, I can hardly believe it.* But you'll be shy at first, shuffling your feet, taking in the vibe, watching the other people smoke, laugh, and relax, in full enjoyment of their freedom. Then you'll think to yourself: *Now what?*

Like the menu at a fancy restaurant, the multitude of offerings at a coffeeshop can be intimidating to the uninitiated. And while it's tempting to assume that anything you order in Amsterdam will be "dam" good, it's not necessarily true, and besides, that's missing the point. You didn't travel across the ocean to simply smoke weed—you've done that at home, many times. You came to Amsterdam to smoke the weed you want, the way you want, and to be treated like a customer instead of a criminal.

Here are some tips to make sure your first time is a Dutch treat.

Ask for a Recommendation. The person behind the counter knows a lot more about what's on the menu than you do, and will be happy to help you make a selection. Mention whether you want hash or cannabis, how much money you're looking to spend, and what kind of effect ("stoned" or "high") you're hoping to achieve. Generally, *indicas* will produce a heavier, more powerful stone, while *sativas* provide a more uplifting high.

Trust Your Senses. It's okay—go ahead and ask to see or smell a strain before purchasing; just don't ask for a free sample to smoke. And kindly refrain from squeezing the Charmin.

Weights and Measures. When it comes time to cough up your money, the price will be in euros and the product will be in grams. Since you're unfamiliar with both these units of measure, and stoned, it can get confusing at checkout time. Consult the exchange rate for "dollars to euros" and see the "ounces to grams" chart on the following page before making a purchase—it's the only way to know what you're really getting for your money.

Buy Nothing Prerolled. If you don't know how to roll a joint, what better place to learn than at a coffeeshop in Amsterdam? If you do know how, you've got no excuse for being so lazy. Either way, any grass you buy in a prerolled spliff will be bottom-of-the-barrel shake the coffeeshop sells off to people who don't know any better. And now you know better.

Buy Something Besides Weed. No, you don't *have* to buy anything else, but it's considered a bit impolite to purchase nothing but Mary Jane, especially if you plan to stay and smoke on the premises. Besides, wouldn't a cup of hot tea with honey feel nice on your throat right about now? And maybe a pastry, and something with chocolate, and . . .

☘ OUNCES TO GRAMS: ☘
A STONER'S CONVERSION CHART

1 pound	455.52 grams
1 ounce	28.47 grams
¼ ounce	7.118 grams
⅛ ounce	3.559 grams
1 kilogram	35.125 ounces

Note: Most American dealers actually weigh out a 448-gram "pound," which is preferred because it's evenly divisible into eighths. Unlike the traditional "baker's dozen," which benefits the consumer with an extra donut, bagel, or pastry, the "dealer's ounce" benefits the house.

Amsterdam's hundreds of cannabis coffeeshops cater to all kinds of customers, with vibes that range from cozy to convivial, so don't get stuck in any one stop for too long.

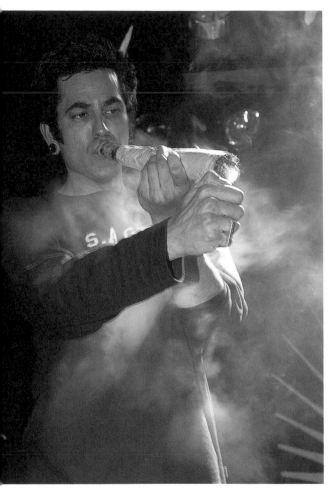

Do not try this at home, unless you've got plenty of weed to burn.

ourselves, and our red eyes grow larger than our lungs. It's a shame, because Amsterdam's a beautiful city, and you're missing out on a lot if you're only seeing it through half-closed lids.

TAKE A SAUNA BREAK

About midway through the Cup, you've got to get yourself into the steam at one of Amsterdam's famous saunas, sweat it all out, and then treat yourself to a massage afterward. The first joint you smoke after leaving the spa will feel as fresh as the first one you had after getting off the plane, and you should be good to go until the Cup's closing ceremony.

STAY OUT OF THE BIKE LANE

They love bicycles in Amsterdam, and you should love them too—they're quiet, they reduce traffic and save fossil fuels, they improve fitness and the environment, and they're fun to ride. In fact, there's no better way to see the city than by renting a bike and taking your own tour. What's not fun, however, is wandering into the bike lane on foot without realizing it, and then getting creamed. No fun at all.

The bike lane is a potential pitfall for every traveler in Amsterdam, but it's a particular problem for the Cannabis Cup crowd. God bless us, but sometimes we walk around with our heads in the clouds, which is all well and good, but first, get out of the bike lane! Seriously, you're gonna get hit!

AVOID TOBACCO MIXES

Odds are, if you live in the United States, you can't get good imported hashish with any regularity. It's getting easier to make your own (see page 194), but that's still a far cry from sampling the international delights offered up in Amsterdam's coffeeshops. So make the most of the opportunity to taste the best of Nepal, Morocco, Kashmir, and other hash hotspots from around the world, but watch out for any joint you didn't roll yourself. Europeans often mix their weed with tobacco, and almost always mix it in when rolling hash.

If you don't normally smoke tobacco, puffing down on one of these "blends" will turn your face the deep green of a late-summer *sativa*, and be a waste of good hash, as well as your lunch. And if you *do* regularly smoke tobacco, you should stop immediately. Sure, it's legal in the United States, but it's also addictive and deadly, unlike cannabis, which is illegal in the United States—one of the reasons you came to Amsterdam in the first place. *Fucked up, isn't it?*

❧ USE THE BUD-DY SYSTEM

No matter what kind of trouble you're getting into in Amsterdam, it'll be a lot easier to get out of if you're rolling with a friend. Two "heads" are truly better than one, after all, whether you're trying to remember the name of your hotel, figuring out how to order pancakes (a local specialty called *pannakoken*), or puzzling over the menu at your first coffeeshop.

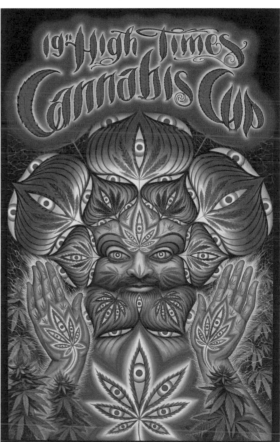

IMPROVE YOUR JAY-DAR *Learn to tell the pot-friendly from the not-friendly in any crowd*

"So, do you ever, you know . . . uh, like to have a smoke?"

It doesn't matter if you're talking to a coworker, a new friend, or even a potential love interest—marijuana can be a tricky subject to broach. Many people live a double life when it comes to Mary Jane, keeping her a secret from all but a few like-minded buds. Others are more open, but still maintain a short list of "those who must never know," which can include anyone from a kindly

Top: *A converted leaf blower fumigates the crowd at the 18th Annual Cannabis Cup.* ABOVE: *Poster art from the 19th Cup.*

old aunt to a parole officer to the head of the P.T.A. In this time of heavy-duty repression and paranoia, nobody can blame anybody for keeping a low profile when it comes to getting high. In fact, this is one of the main goals of marijuana prohibition: to keep us freethinkers from getting together and thinking up a better way to be free.

Still, there are certain times when you make a new acquaintance, and you're just sure that other person would be happy as a clambake if you pulled out your stash and started rolling one up. And so there you are: You've got some great weed and you're more than willing to share—the only problem is that inevitable *What if . . . ?*

What if this hottie I'm dancing with at my cousin's wedding not only doesn't want to take bong hits in the parking lot, but decides to turn me in to her father the federal agent instead? What if the other caddy where I work not only doesn't want to split a blunt in the clump of trees near the fifth green, but he narcs on me to the boss and gets me fired? What if the babysitter does not appreciate being tipped with a fat joint?

If only there was some obvious way for pot smokers to signal their "green light" status to one another. Much like homosexuals, who claim to have *gay-dar*, we heads must hone our own *jay-dar*, so we can combat the tactic of divide and conquer that has kept us in the closet for the past seventy years. Now, admittedly, many of us grow weed in our closets, but high-pressure sodium lights are a poor substitute for pure sunshine, so here are a few helpful hints on how to hone your jay-dar and find the herb smokers in your midst.

 PHYSICAL APPEARANCE

Sherlock Holmes could draw the most elaborate deductions from simply observing the appearance of a person who entered his flat. You should do some detective work of your own. Look carefully for the following clues, any one of which should set your jay-dar tingling: dreadlocks, tie-dye, hemp, yellowing of thumb and forefinger, red eyes, droopy lids, dry lips, wide smile, cornrows, Birkenstocks, rasta colors, yoga mat, skateboard, beard, tattoos, guitar case . . .

 VERBAL CUES

Dude, if someone says "dude" a lot, then, "fucking *dude*"—that's a good sign. Listen carefully for the stoner's telltale conversational pause, the likelihood of repeating a good story more than thrice, and casual mention of any of the many, many monikers marijuana goes by—everything from muggles to Mary Jane. Also, don't be afraid to drop a few well-placed hints of your own, which can be accomplished with a minimum of risk. For instance, if they don't smoke 'dro, then they won't know what you're talking about when you ask them to pass it. **Warning:** The word is out on 420, so beware when interacting with the straight world— they have cracked our code. Please remain calm and continue to smoke as you would normally.

 CULTURAL REFERENCES

"Hey, do you like Bob Marley?" you might ask someone at a party. And if they say, *"Why yes, I do like Bob Marley,"* then you add, "I think I just saw him step outside—want to help me look for him?"

Other cultural references to keep in mind: Willie Nelson, beat poetry, hydroponics, jazz music, Pantera, forestry, *Dazed and Confused*, Cypress Hill, and lava lamps.

✹ LEADING QUESTIONS

"Hey, do you smell reefer?"

✹ THE DIRECT APPROACH

"Mind if I light this joint?"

FOOD FOR THOUGHT *Never bite off more ganja food than you can chew, dude . . .*

Marijuana is meant to be eaten, and as anyone who's ever attempted an outdoor grow can attest, we humans are far from the only species to find pot a delicacy. Mold and fungus live off the herb. Many insects feast on it. Even bears have been found peacefully stoned and snoozing in the middle of some poor cultivator's clandestine little clearing in the woods, resting up after having wrecked a season's worth of work in one fell swoop. (If this ever happens to you, by the way, it's best to cut your losses and just let the bear sleep it off. You can always come back the next day to salvage whatever wasn't eaten or trampled. As an old Native American proverb cautions: *He who stands between a bear and his grass soon runs for his life*.)

Also, always remember that the high you get from eating pot is more physical, powerful, and psychedelic than the one you get from smoking.

Always measure the secret ingredient carefully when cooking with cannabis.

Sometimes the uninitiated (like our hypothetical bear) find themselves literally knocked off their asses. It's not dangerous, but it ain't pretty, either. In fact, some of the coffeeshops in Amsterdam have stopped serving space cake, hash brownies, and other THC–laden treats because of the occasional meltdowns that result.

A typical bad scene goes down something like this:

"Wow, holy shit, pot brownies. Amsterdam is the *best*! I'll buy enough for everyone, and we can split them up when we meet for lunch. Then we'll hit the Van Gogh museum, followed by a long walk through Vondel Park."

"I should try a little taste of this brownie, to test them."

"Man, that was yummy. And I'm totally stoned from that bong I smoked back at the coffeeshop. Maybe a few more bites would be okay."

"It's been fifteen minutes since I ate that brownie. I don't feel anything. I should have another one, just to make sure I didn't get ripped off . . . and oh, what the hell, maybe one more. At least they *taste* good."

"Wow, all the names of all the streets in Amsterdam sure do look alike. So many consonants. So precious few vowels. I wonder if I made a wrong turn back there . . ."

"Where was I supposed to meet the guys again? And isn't that just what they're *expecting* me to do?"

"Is *lunch* really a word, or am I making it up?"

Where things go from there is anybody's guess, but let's just say you don't end up making that appointment for lunch, you don't see any of the paintings in the Van Gogh museum, and the long walk through Vondel Park ends on a park bench, where you spend the next few hours with yesterday's newspaper draped over your head, muttering the *Green Acres* theme song and slowly returning to normal.

So what went awry? First off, you forgot about a little something called the digestive system. It takes at least thirty minutes, and sometimes as long as two hours, to start feeling the effects of ganja food, depending on how strong it is, what else you've been eating, and the many subtleties of the human mind. The experience will then grow steadily more intense for a few hours before gradually receding. So start with a little taste and see what happens. You can always eat more later.

BUDDER UP

Once you know how to make ganja butter ("budder"), you know how to make pot-infused foods that will send your flight crew into the stratosphere. Simply follow your favorite recipes, replacing plain old butter with the stuff you've infused in advance with an oh-so-special secret ingredient. Of course, you can always just spread your "budder" on a piece of toast to make things easy, but what's the fun in that?

For that matter, yes, you can simply eat buds straight off the stem until you get high, but it will

Never dump your herb right into the brownie mix! For best results, follow our simple "budder" recipe instead.

take a lot of chewing and cost a ton of money, because when you eat "raw" marijuana, your stomach can only absorb a small portion of the THC and other cannabinoids in the plant. You need to give those molecules something to bind onto, which means the most efficient way of ingesting cannabis resins involves slowly simmering the buds and leaves in something with a high fat content, like butter, cream, or oil.

That's why you should never let someone tell you that it's okay to simply grind up your buds and put them right in the brownie batter, *dude*, as this is a recipe for disaster. Instead, follow the simple ganja butter directions below, and you'll soon be famous for your mesmerizing marijuana meals and potent pot pastries. For inspiration, we've included a few of our staff's favorite recipes for your consideration, all of which made their debut as part of a little tradition called Space Cake Friday.

GANJA BUTTER

1 stick butter
⅛ to ¼ ounce ground cannabis buds

Combine butter and ganja in a double boiler over low heat for 45 minutes, stirring frequently. Strain out the plant matter and then use the "infused" butter in any recipe that calls for it, careful to measure your dosage.

POT LUCK High Times' *ganja gourmets offer up their best recipes*

If you want to become famous among your friends for your cannabis-containing culinary creations, you can follow two distinct paths. The first is to produce pot-laden treats so powerful that even the distinct taste of dried bongwater does not diminish their overall appeal enough to keep your crew from choking them down and then waiting patiently for the thrill ride to follow. The other path requires a bit more work, including learning to bake, cook, fry, sauté, or otherwise whip up something good enough to stand on the shelf of the finest gourmet shop, if not for the not-so-secret ingredient concealed within all that deliciousness. Regrettably, these two talents seldom seem to dovetail. When it comes time to put our marijuana where our mouth is and eat it too, the tainted treats always seem to arrive as either some godawful, sand-dry brownie, which—despite being nearly inedible—nonetheless sends you into orbit, or, conversely, as an unbelievably delicious high-quality cannabis confection that—while tasty and well-meaning—doesn't exactly pack the required punch.

So when these appropriately named Coconut Magic Bars (see page 58) mysteriously appeared, made by a friend of *High Times* from an old family recipe, we were somewhat skeptical. They looked great and tasted even better . . . but would they work? The answer arrived two hours later, when we collectively decided to type out the meaning of life (which we'd just collectively discovered) and mail it to ourselves so we wouldn't forget.

Unfortunately we ended up sending it off to the wrong address by mistake.

No worries, though—all we need to do is follow the recipe and we should be back in touch with nirvana in no time flat.

COCONUT MAGIC BARS

3 sticks butter

1 cup finely ground cannabis

4½ cups graham cracker crumbs

2 cups chopped walnuts

1 cup mini butterscotch chips

4½ cups sweetened, shredded coconut

3 fourteen-ounce cans sweetened condensed milk

1.   Preheat oven to 325 degrees F.

2.   To make the butter, melt the 3 sticks of butter over a low heat, and when almost melted, slowly add in the ground cannabis. Let simmer

Warning: Coconut Magic Bars may play tricks on your mind.

for approximately 45 minutes, stirring occasionally. Strain out plant matter.

3.   To make the crust, in a large bowl combine the graham cracker crumbs with the melted butter. Press firmly into the bottom of a 12-by-18-inch pan.

4.   Fill the center with a layer of walnuts, then add a layer of butterscotch chips, followed by a layer of shredded coconut. Pour the sweetened, condensed milk over the top.

5.   Bake 30 to 35 minutes or until golden brown. *Stones 8–10.*

🌿 GOO BALLS

A short walk down Shakedown Street reveals that there are as many different recipes for goo balls out there as there are enthusiastic hippies in dreadlocks hawking wicker baskets full of these round, sweet treats for cash, trade, or your extra. Like the improvisational music scene that attracts the fans who go in for these ganja-laden parking-lot staples, the goo ball represents more of a template for bold experimentation than a strict recipe to be followed. Sometimes we've found organic nut-clusterish granola-style balls that were delicious but to little psychoactive effect, and on other occasions we've been handed a small lump of chunky store-brand peanut butter with some Fruity Pebbles and raisins hanging off it and ended up spending the second set dancing shirtless and barefoot in the rain.

High Times recommends purchasing at least two different treats per show, in the hope that at least one of them will possess the empowering dose of ganja-infused goodness promised by the aforementioned hippie with wicker basket.

Of course, the only way to completely ensure that your goo balls are all they can be is to make them yourself, to suit your own taste. So find the recipe that's right for you, or better yet make one up as you go along. Just jam on it, man—really explore the kitchen space—and then add the kind and amount of ganja butter that's going to keep you grooving like you've never grooved before.

COCOBERRY GANJA GOO BALLS

⅓ cup canola oil

6 to 12 grams finely ground cannabis buds
    and leaves

¾ cup shredded coconut

¼ cup sweet cocoa powder

¼ cup sesame tahini

¼ cup peanut butter

⅓ cup sunflower seeds

¾ cup dried cranberries (or raisins)

3 teaspoons vanilla extract

1 teaspoon cinnamon

½ cup powdered sugar

1. Heat the canola oil in a wok or heavy saucepan. Stir in the cannabis, and simmer, stirring often, for 20 minutes or until plant matter is crispy.

2. Strain out particulates carefully and set oil aside. In a large mixing bowl, combine ¼ cup of the coconut and the sweet cocoa

The tastiest, most potent Goo Balls always arrive in a wicker basket.

powder. Add the sesame tahini, peanut butter, and cannabis oil, using a whisk if necessary to blend ingredients thoroughly.

3. Add sunflower seeds, cranberries, and the remaining coconut, followed by the vanilla extract and cinnamon. The mixture will still have a soupy consistency. Slowly stir in the powdered sugar until the mixture has thickened. Oils need some time to be absorbed, so allow mixture to sit for 10 minutes.

4. Cover a baking sheet in wax paper. Form batter into balls and freeze on baking sheet for several hours. Serve chilled. *Stones 8.*

HOW TO SMOKE-PROOF
YOUR DORM ROOM

There's no better and no worse place to smoke weed than a college dorm room. Ah, the wonderful cramped, stinky, cell-like dorm room. It's a special place to live during a very special time in your life, and as every coed knows, every floor in every dorm has one super special room, usually down at the end of the hall: The Puff Palace. The Smoke Stack. The Burn Center. Whatever your own pet nickname, it's the marijuana smoking room, and odds are, if you bought this book, it's your room.

People constantly break the law on your futon, and you want to keep them (not to mention yourself) safe, so what's the best method to prevent some authoritarian smoke detector from knocking on your door? High Times, *like life, offers no guarantees, only a few suggestions, plus the pros and cons of various smoke-reduction strategies. Whatever your method, the most important thing to remember is due diligence. So good luck, happy smoking, and for God's sake, clean your sheets once in a while.*

THE FIVE COMMANDMENTS OF DORM ROOM SMOKING SAFETY

1. THOU SHALT NOT OPEN THE DOOR DURING A SESSION Sorry, but if you're in, you're in for the duration, and if you're out, you're shit out of luck. Announce a "countdown to burndown" five minutes prior to toking to make sure the whole cannabis crew is assembled before sparking up, and be sure to let things air out for at least fifteen minutes after the last exhale before opening the door.

2. THOU SHALT SESH, NOT STEW Smoke 'em if you got 'em, and then let things clear out a bit (in your room and in your head).

3. THOU SHALT KEEP IT DOWN, DUDE Yup, you're stoned, and it's a funny story, but you can't be gettin' all loud about it and drawing unwanted attention. This, of course, goes double for nocturnal nuggets.

4. THOU SHALL KEEP THE JOINTS TO A MINIMUM There's just no smokier way to smoke than the joint. Blunts, at least, have a tobacco masking, but they're still troublemakers (especially in a "smoke-free" room). Remember, even when you're not puffing, that joint is smoking away in your hand . . .

5. THOU SHALT NOT GET ALL PARANOID AND SHIT If you're taking proper precautions, there's no reason to freak out. It's a classic buzzkill, and you're better than that. *Wait—turn down the music . . . did you just hear some voices in the hallway?*

SMOKESCREENS: *HIGH TIMES* REVIEWS SEVEN POPULAR STRATEGIES FOR STONER SCENT REDUCTION

	ADVANTAGES	*DISADVANTAGES*
MUTES	Cheaply made from dryer sheets and a paper-towel roll. Effective at the point of usage.	They don't work unless you actually blow the smoke into them. After the first trip around the circle, your forgetful friends will expose this basic design flaw.
FANS	Disperse smoke rapidly through air circulation. Also, it's sometimes cool to turn them off and watch the whirring blades slowly wind down.	Unless properly aligned, they can backfire, pushing a fragrant trade wind out your door and into the hallway. Consult one of the physics majors from your dorm on how to tailor a system to your needs.
SPRAYS	Mask the pot smell nicely, as well as the stench from your "laundry pile." We suggest baking powder–based scents.	Some paranoid person will invariably grab the can and go apeshit on it. Your room will then reek of Mountainberry Seascape Potpourri for the next 18 hours.
CIGARETTES	The powerful, socially acceptable stench of tobacco effectively covers the sweet, life-affirming scent of cannabis.	They will slowly kill you, after decades of expensive addiction.
INCENSE	Nice smell. Can be stolen from church.	"You're not fooling anyone with that incense, by the way," a common expression since 1972.
TOWEL UNDER THE DOOR	Prevents people from entering or leaving the room (see Commandment #1, opposite page). Also, couldn't hurt.	Relying on the towel alone is like using the rhythm method for birth control. It might work for a while, but roll the dice enough times and eventually you're going to lose.
IONIZER	Magically clears air through some science related process.	If you had the money for an ionizer, you'd just buy more weed with it anyway.

Redman enjoyed our Peanut Butter Hash Fudge so much he followed us to Amsterdam for the 20th Annual Cannabis Cup.

EASY BAKE: REDMAN DISAPPEARS WITH HIS FAVORITE HASH FUDGE

"Ya'll know how to get high," Redman commented approvingly upon biting into a piece of delicious ganja-infused peanut butter fudge. "This is fucking bananas."

No bananas in the recipe, you'll notice, but Redman's point remains well taken: Good ganja food can be an unexpected treat for even the most seasoned stoners among us. In this case, an incredibly simple dish we whipped up in just a few minutes ended up adding a sugar rush of excitement to a *High Times* photo shoot that brought together two of the biggest heads in the hip-hop universe

for an herb-filled few hours. And while Method Man clearly prefers smoking to snacking, and only sampled a bite or two to be polite, Redman couldn't get enough of our hash-powered fudge. He even took the leftovers with him when he left. *All* the leftovers.

Not that he didn't leave us laughing. Red had us in stitches by the time we wrapped—pretending he was talking into his shoe phone, running around wearing a crazy fake beard supplied by his personal barber, and even singing to the live plant we brought along for the photo shoot as he watered it. All the while, we wondered: Was the fudge to "blame" for these unscripted antics? If so, then long live the fudge.

Now, you must be thinking: *Good for you guys, sounds like a fun day, but what about me? Where's my fudge?* Very simple: it's in the microwave. Okay, it's not in there yet, but it will be just as soon as you get your hands on some butter, vanilla, peanut butter, powdered sugar, and something that gets you stoned. The only culinary skills you'll need to pull off this cannabis confection is the ability to melt a few things and then mix them together—we're pretty sure you can handle it, even if you've already sampled the secret ingredient before getting started.

So the next time you have a few friends over for THC, why not surprise them with a little something they can sink their sweet teeth into?

PEANUT BUTTER HASH FUDGE

3.5 grams hash (or ganja)
1 cup butter, plus more for greasing pan
1 cup peanut butter

1 teaspoon vanilla extract

1 pound powdered sugar

1. Finely grind the hash and fluff with lighter before combining with the 1 cup butter and the peanut butter in a microwave-safe bowl. Microwave on high for 2 minutes.

2. Stir, making sure hash dissolves completely, then microwave on high for 2 more minutes. Add the vanilla and powdered sugar and mix thoroughly with a wooden spoon.

3. Pour into a buttered pan lined with waxed paper. Place a second piece of waxed paper on the surface of the fudge and refrigerate until cool.

4. Cut into 1-inch pieces and store in an airtight container for up to a week. *Stones 8–12.*

❧ MORE BHANG FOR YOUR BUCK

Bhang's not only good enough to whip up as an offering to Lord Shiva (see "Highstory," page 12), but this divinely delicious cannabis concoction also makes the most of your marijuana dollar by literally squeezing every last drop of THC out of your buds and leaves. Try this traditional recipe and you may find that *bhang*'s not only more economical than smoking, but also more spiritual.

BHANG

2 cups water

1 ounce marijuana (fresh leaves and flowers
     of a female plant preferred)

4 cups warm milk

2 tablespoons blanched chopped almonds

⅛ teaspoon garam masala (a mixture of
     cloves, cinnamon, and cardamom)

¼ teaspoon powdered ginger

½ to 1 teaspoon rosewater

1 cup sugar

1. Bring the water to a rapid boil and pour into a clean teapot. Remove any seeds or twigs from the marijuana, add it to the teapot, and cover.

2. Let this brew steep for about 7 minutes. Strain the "tea" through a piece of muslin cloth into a bowl, squeezing the leaves and flowers with your hands to extract any remaining liquid.

3. Place the leaves and flowers in a mortar and add 2 teaspoons of the warm milk. Slowly but firmly grind the milk and leaves together. Remove the marijuana and squeeze out as much milk as you can into a separate bowl.

4. Repeat this process until you have used about ½ cup of the milk (about 4 to 5 times). By this time the marijuana will have turned into a pulpy mass.

5. Add the chopped almonds to the marijuana pulp and some more warm milk, and grind in the mortar until a fine paste is formed. Squeeze the liquid from the paste and add it to the milk as before. Repeat a few more times until all that is left are some fibers and nut meal. Discard this residue.

6. Combine the milk with the marijuana water and add the garam masala, powdered ginger, and rosewater to taste. Stir in the sugar and remaining milk. Chill. *Stones 12–15.*

CHEAT SHEET *If you have to take a drug test, might as well pass . . .*

The first thing you need to know about drug tests is that they're total bullshit—an invasion of privacy that merely registers the presence of drugs in your system, not impairment, which means they draw no distinction between smoking a joint at home on a Friday night and smoking crack while driving the school bus. And the biggest bullshit of all? The hard stuff (coke, heroin, alcohol) leaves your body in a matter of days, if not hours, while freeloading, couch-surfing marijuana can crash out in your fat cells for a month or more.

If you find yourself facing a piss test, your odds of success depend on three factors: How long until the test; how long since you last smoked; and how much and how often you have smoked over the past thirty days. Whatever the answers, rest assured that just as there's a $6 billion-per-year drug-test industry profiting off all this bullshit, there's also a "drug test solutions" industry offering products to help you cheat your way to a brand-new job.

Simply find a company you trust and visit their Web site for more information on their products. And don't feel guilty in the least: If someone has the nerve to ask for your urine, they deserve what you hand them!

 ## PISS TIPS: HOW TO PASS THE ONE TEST YOU CAN'T STUDY FOR

The best way to pass a drug test is to put time between getting high and unzipping your fly. Most drug test solution products insist on a minimum 48- to 72-hour window of abstinence before the test. THC appears in urine 2 to 4 hours after smoking, and may persist in detectable amounts for up to thirty days. Secondhand marijuana smoke should not cause a positive urine-test result.

Drink as much water as possible in the days leading up to the test, to flush your system. THC can also be sweated out of the body.

Urinate as much as possible at home before arriving for your drug test. Avoid giving the urine at the beginning and end of your stream.

If you use a "drug test solution," follow all manufacturer's recommendations exactly. If you use a device concealing "clean" urine, practice using it at home before the day of the test.

SET YOUR VAPORIZERS FOR STONE

Like *High Times* magazine, the concept of vaporizing marijuana dates back to the 1970s. In those heady days, gadget-minded potheads would rig up do-it-yourself vaporization systems that may have been a bit crude, but they certainly got the job done. Today, more than a dozen different vaporizer companies compete in a rapidly growing product market, with some models priced fairly cheap and some costing hundreds of dollars, but still, most stoners have never tried it. And that's a shame.

When you burn a joint, you inhale not only THC and cannabinoids—marijuana's "active" ingredients—but also smoke resulting from burning the surrounding plant matter. Both scientific studies and anecdotal evidence have shown that marijuana smoke is not harmful to your lungs in any way approaching the harm of tobacco, but nonetheless, vaporizing offers a healthier alternative to smoking for medical marijuana patients and anyone with an existing respiratory condition.

The simplest vaporizers use a cigarette lighter for heat, and the most advanced plug into the wall or run off a battery. All of them work by heating marijuana to around 365 degrees Fahrenheit, the temperature at which the resinous glands will melt into a light vapor with a scent more akin to the flowery smell of fresh ganja than the sweet, heavy aroma of marijuana smoke. Those oily resin glands contain both the plant's THC and other cannibinoids, and since they're released at a lower temperature than that at which the plant burns, their vapor can be extracted free from any contaminating smoke. Not only does this result in a lighter load for your lungs, vaporizing marijuana also makes more efficient use of your stash, produces a wonderfully fragrant taste, and often results in a clearer, more cerebral high.

Convection systems, in which hot air flows over the marijuana, are most effective, and the best models feature temperature control and easy to-use inhalation devices ranging from plastic tubing to bong-like attachments to inflating bags

These girls run the Cannabis College in Amsterdam, so rest assured, they're experts in the fine art of vaporization.

that can be detached from the system and passed around like a joint.

Less advanced conduction systems heat metal, which transfers this heat directly to the marijuana. These systems are less efficient and fragrant, but cheaper and easier to build yourself.

High price tags, inconvenience, and unfamiliarity have kept the vaporizer out of the average stoner's hands since its invention, but costs are coming down, and the newer models are far more user-friendly. At the 17th Annual *High Times* Cannabis Cup in 2005, the opening ceremonies included a 21-vaporizer salute that likely won a few converts to the world of vaporization.

SHOTGUN!

The concept originated among U.S. soldiers in Vietnam, who sometimes smoked the plentiful local *sativas* out of their shotguns by fitting

Soldiers in Vietnam sometimes smoked the local sativas *out of modified shotguns.*

a loaded pipe into the chamber, lighting it, and having one soldier blow the smoke from the pipe down to his buddy waiting at the business end of the weapon. Nowadays, the same concept can still be applied, albeit without the actual shotgun. The shotgunner simply puts a smoking joint into his mouth backward, holding the lit end inside so that it doesn't burn his lips. The "shotgunned" then inhales from the unlit end at the same time his buddy exhales in the opposite direction. Warning: The results may blow your mind.

A COOL, DARK PLACE

Okay, you went off and got yourself some weed. You rolled some, you smoked some, and you passed it on the left-hand side—all very good. But what about the rest of your stash? For best results, store your dried herbs in an airtight container that's large enough not to crush them, and then hide it in a cool, dark place. Most important, don't forget

your hiding place. Yes, it happens, and the ensuing search is a very frustrating way to waste an afternoon.

HOOKAH ME UP, BROTHER!

Take a trip to ancient Arabia without leaving your living room by loading up one of these ornamental pipes. Featuring water filtration, stems for several heads to puff at once, and a bed of burning coals to indirectly heat the smokeables, the hookah originated with the Arabs, and made its way around the world via the Ottoman Empire, usually stuffed with hashish.

Despite enforcing an all-out ban on alcohol, the Koran makes no prohibition against cannabis, and so proper hookah smoking enjoys a long history in the Islamic world. Unfortunately, hashish is currently outlawed by the government everywhere in the region, but the hookah, now filled with tobacco and fruits (at least in public), nevertheless remains an integral part of social life in that part of the world.

Meanwhile, in America, headshops will usually carry a hookah or two, but you can find the best deals on the most authentic pieces by locating the nearest Middle Eastern neighborhood and taking a field trip. Don't mention marijuana to the store owner, but do feel free to ask a few questions, like where the pipes come from and what customs smokers follow in those regions. This way you'll have a few interesting tidbits to relate the first time you break out the hookah.

Chapter 3

POT CULTURE

Most major potheads can't fathom attending a concert or watching a movie without partaking of some marijuana first. Not only does a "pre-game" session enhance our art appreciation, it also helps us reach the same mental wavelength as the pot-smoking artists who created all that art in the first place.

The link between getting high and high art likely stretches back all the way to the earliest herb-smoking drummers in Africa, and although those prehistoric sessions were unfortunately not recorded, we stoners do have countless albums, books, movies, paintings, comix, and videogames to call our own. And that's just the marijuana masterpieces we know about. Recently, archeological research on cannabis resin in a pipe found buried in Stratford-upon-Avon, England, led to conjecture that William Shakespeare himself might have been "imbibing the emerald flowers," so to speak, while writing his most famous plays. We'll never know for sure about Shakespeare, but the first time that five of the 20th century's most influential artists met, marijuana undoubtedly broke the ice—not to mention changed music forever.

In 1964, the Beatles were touring America for the first time. They still hadn't encountered cannabis, and, not coincidentally, considered it in a class alongside heroin and other hard drugs. When the tour reached New York City, however, a timely visit from Bob Dylan would change their minds, in more ways than one.

After enduring a police and bodyguard escort through all the Beatlemania surrounding the band's inner sanctum, Dylan finally arrived at Manhattan's posh Delmonico Hotel armed with enough

John Lennon Reveals . . .

The Beatles Were 'High' on Marijuana When Queen Elizabeth Decorated Them At Buckingham Palace

GEORGE HARRISON
1970

JOHN LENNON
1970

PAUL McCARTNEY
1970

QUEEN ELIZABETH
Awarded medals

RINGO STARR
1970

By THOMAS KNOWLES

The Beatles smoked marijuana right under the staid noses of the British royal family — in Buckingham Palace.

"We smoked a 'joint' in the lavatory of the palace because we were nervous about meeting the Queen," admitted John Lennon, the group's most outspoken member, in an interview in Paris.

The incident took place in 1965 when the Beatles were invited to the official residence of Queen Elizabeth and her family to receive an honor award, the MBE.

Lennon's recent "pot in the palace" confession has outraged the conservative British almost as much as the original announcement that the long-haired pop group would receive the decoration.

The MBE — Member of the Order of the British Empire — is traditionally awarded by the reigning monarch for distinguished service to the country.

"When we heard we had been recommended for the MBE, I took it as a joke and at first we wanted to laugh," Lennon said.

"But once it happens, when you actually receive your decoration you don't make jokes any longer.

"But we giggled all the same — you see, we had just smoked a joint (marijuana cigarette) in the lavatory at Buckingham Palace. We were high and so nervous . . ."

Lennon said the four Beatles were overawed by the lavish surroundings, and at coming face-to-face with the Queen.

"Even if you don't believe in royalty you can't help being impressed," he said.

Lennon said he wanted to refuse the MBE at first but was talked into accepting the prestige award by their manager. Lennon has since sent his back. Lennon recalled that the Beatles were using drugs when they made their film, "Help."

"The best scenes were those when we were sprawling on the floor unable to say a word.

"We'd just started to smoke marijuana and we were stoned."

He admitted also that the Beatles were on "acid" or LSD when they cut their best-selling LP, "Sergeant Pepper."

After making these admissions the 29-year-old Lennon said he no longer believed in taking drugs.

"The ideal is to have no drugs at all, no coffee, no cigarettes, no drinks. I gave up cigarettes but I started again, it was too hard to go without.

"But I'm against drugs, I really am."

HONORED: Happy Beatles (from left) Ringo Starr, John Lennon, Paul McCartney and George Harrison display medals presented to them by Queen Elizabeth.

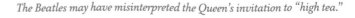

The Beatles may have misinterpreted the Queen's invitation to "high tea."

weed to roll at least a dozen joints. Bob reached John, Paul, George, and Ringo just as they finished a room-service dinner, and after some awkward introductions, he offered to roll up something from Mother Earth.

When the Beatles explained that they didn't smoke grass, Dylan was dumbfounded. He had misheard John Lennon's lyrics on "I Want to Hold Your Hand" ("I can't hide" as "I get high"), and assumed the song was in praise of marijuana. Finally, a bit in awe of Dylan's talent and renown as a serious songwriter, the decidedly teenybopper Beatles took a unanimous vote and decided to give it a go. Ringo served as "royal taster," smoking the entire first joint Dylan rolled before breaking into hysterical laughter and passing along his endorsement to the remaining Fab Four.

The rest, as they say, is highstory. Dylan, already tagged the "voice of a generation," became one of the most important and enduring artists of our time, while the freshly turned-on Beatles soon stopped touring to screaming girls and instead focused on crafting a string of brilliant albums that would transform four pop sensations into worldwide ambassadors for peace, love, and pot.

Not bad for a bunch of stoners, right?

---

20 SONGS FOR 420

Selecting twenty all-time top pot songs required a lot of smoking and a lot of listening, because over the years so many amazing musicians have sung the praises of Mary Jane. Our highly subjective list includes tracks from the earliest days of jazz, the roots days of reggae, the outlaw days of country, the psychedelic days of rock, the heavy days of metal, the groovy days of funk, and the old-school days of hip-hop. The musicians on our list represent not only the cream of the cannabis crop, but some of the most respected and revered artists of all time.

Roll it all together and you've got the stoniest playlist imaginable.

🌿 **1. "KAYA"** *Bob Marley (1978)* Bob Marley sang about his love and respect for ganja proudly and often, on tracks ranging from "Three Little Birds," a mellow song about a trio of feathered friends who would gather outside his doorstep to eat the seeds discarded from his morning spliff, to the frustration and defiance of "Three O'Clock in the Morning (Roadblock)," about having to toss away his "little herb stalk" when faced with a random police traffic stop.

To Rastafarians, *kaya* means enlightenment, and is often used as slang for marijuana. On the title track from his 1978 album, Marley extols the virtues of having a "wake and bake" on a rainy morning.

🌿 **2. "RAINY DAY WOMEN #12 & 35"** *Bob Dylan (1966)* Better known for its refrain of "Everybody must get stoned" than for its somewhat puzzling title, Dylan's homage to herb cleverly plays off the other meaning of getting stoned, the biblical punishment involving the collective village throwing rocks at you until you die. Still, even the

Reggae in Kingston—the New Nashville!

High Times

September '76

$1.50

Michael Stepanian— San Francisco's Dope Superlawyer

Tom Robbins' New Novel— Even Cowgirls Get the Blues

Paul Bowles on Kif *plus* **Exclusive Moroccan Kif-Making Photos**

Comix: Reality, Perception and Donuts

Dreadful Special A Spectacular Doper's Guide to Jamaica

How to: Roll the Best Spliffs Speak the Rasta Lingo Find the Highest Ganja Look that Dreadlock Look

Peter Tosh on Holy Smokes

Will Jamaica Be the Stoned Cuba?

Marley Speaks!

Bob Marley

The Herb

squares knew what Dylan was *really* talking about, which meant the song was banned from the radio despite reaching #2 on the charts. And by the way, 12 x 35 = 420 . . .

🌿 3. "REEFER MAN" *Cab Calloway (1932)*

Cab Calloway recorded this tongue-in-cheek tribute to marijuana dealers five years before "the devil's lettuce" was made illegal—a time when most Americans still hadn't even heard of marijuana ("Have you ever met this funny reefer man / If he trades you dimes for nickels and calls watermelons pickles, then you know you're talkin' to that reefer man").

🌿 4. "LEGALIZE IT" *Peter Tosh (1976)*

Once a member of the Wailers alongside Bob Marley, Peter Tosh embarked on a highly political solo career after leaving the band, including this anthemic call to change the marijuana laws ("Legalize it / Don't criticize it / Legalize it, and I will advertise it"). Never afraid to voice his opposition to hypocritical governments, both in Jamaica and around the world, Tosh once smoked a spliff onstage during a concert attended by the Prime Minister of Jamaica while demanding the legalization of cannabis.

🌿 5. "GOT TO GET YOU INTO MY LIFE"

The Beatles (1966) There's no overt mention of marijuana in what Paul McCartney later admitted was "an ode to pot" ("I was alone, I took a ride, I didn't know what I would find there"), but rest assured that Sir Paul sings of Mary Jane in this otherwise straightahead love song. And if you're wondering if that love endured, consider this: In 1980, McCartney was arrested and imprisoned for nine days after attempting to bring over seven ounces of herb into Japan.

🌿 6. "HOW TO ROLL A BLUNT" *Redman*

(1992) Named for an instructional *High Times* centerfold (see pages 74–75), this hip-hop classic took the art of blunt rolling to new heights—and new heads. Lately, Redman's been into hanging with his favorite magazine, explaining that after hosting our 2006 Doobie Awards, "Redman is an official *High Times* member."

🌿 7. "AND IT STONED ME" *Van Morrison*

(1970) Van the Man hit it big with this simple song about taking a fishing trip, hitchhiking, and then waiting out the rain with the help of Mary Jane. By the way, *jellyroll* is an old bit of jazz slang for a woman's private parts, so when Van says, "It stoned me just like jellyroll," you'd better believe that was some good weed.

🌿 8. "SWEET LEAF" *Black Sabbath (1971)*

Before he became fodder for the reality TV circuit, Ozzy was the thinking man's badass and a dedicated pothead to boot. In 1999, he posed for the cover of *High Times*, explaining in his interview: "We used to smoke pounds of the shit, man. We used to buy it by the fuckin' sackful."

Muggs taught us how to get blunted.
introduced him to it. All you need to roll a blu
of the buddha (about

I *Bite off the tip of the blunt.*

3 *Peel the outside layer of tobacco off the blunt. If you leave the outside layer on, it tends to have a nasty taste. The single layer doesn't override the nice buddha flavor. Lick the ends of the blunt paper. Wave it in the air, so it'll dry.*

L A BLUNT

Real

...n East Coast thing—one of his friends
... Phillies blunt cigar and a decent quantity
...hth of an oz).

2 *Make a good slice down the middle of the blunt [length-wise]. Either do it by hand or with a razor blade.*

4 *Break up the buddha. Word up. Throw away the tobacco. We don't put that in there, we're not in Europe.*

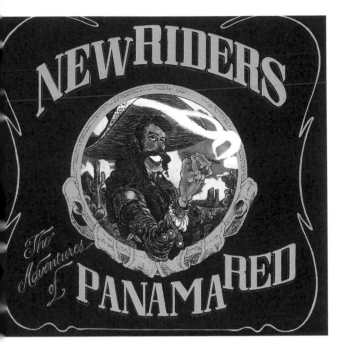

Mary Jane has served as a muse to many of the world's most famous musicians.

🌿 **9. "I WANT TO TAKE YOU HIGHER"** *Sly & the Family Stone (1969)* Released the year of the moon landing and brilliantly performed at Woodstock, this jubilant anthem embodied the yearning of an entire generation of young potheads that wanted to turn on everyone in the world and show them all a new, and "higher," way to live.

🌿 **10. "MARY JANE"** *Rick James (1978)* Today he's best known for Dave Chappelle's impersonation, but before all the cocaine and super-freaky girls caught up with him, Rick James recorded one of the funkiest torch songs of all time ("Do you love me, Mary Jane?").

🌿 **11. "MUGGLES"** *Louis Armstrong (1928)* Long before Harry Potter, *muggles* was slang among jazz musicians for marijuana. Eighty years after it was recorded, this instrumental tribute to toking still sounds amazing when you're baked.

🌿 **12. "ONE TOKE OVER THE LINE"** *Brewer & Shipley (1971)* The highest-charting pot tune of the '70s describes the sensation of puffing tough and suddenly finding yourself in the middle of a crowded train station with a bit too much herb on your mind, "sittin' downtown in a railway station, one toke over the line . . ."

🌿 **13. "I LIKE MARIJUANA"** *David Peel (1968)* *The Pope Smokes Dope*, one of the most incendiary albums of all time, was produced by John Lennon and Yoko Ono, after they met Peel by chance in

New York's Washington Square Park. But first the legendary marijuana minstrel wrote this enduring ditty in support of the stoner lifestyle ("I like marijuana / You like marijuana / We like marijuana too"). By the way, Peel still lives in the Baked Apple and occasionally shows up in Central Park to lead the *High Times* Bonghitters softball team through a stony postgame rendition of his composition "Take Me Out to the Bong Game."

❦ **14. "PANAMA RED"** *New Riders of the Purple Sage (1973)* Once upon a time, the best weed in the world came from South America, including the legendary strain with the dark red hairs that lends its name to this tale of a charming pot smuggler and the women who love him.

❦ **15. "DON'T BOGART ME"** *Fraternity of Man (1969)* An instant classic after its inclusion in the movie *Easy Rider*, this is the timeless lament of the guy standing at the other end of the circle, watching helplessly as someone else takes toke after toke. "Bogarting" refers to film actor Humphrey Bogart, who famously appeared on screen with a cigarette perpetually dangling from the corner of his mouth.

❦ **16. "STONED IS THE WAY OF THE WALK"** *Cypress Hill (1991)* Their first "hit" in more ways than one, the higher-than-high Cypress Hill initially inhaled fame with this ganja-soaked ode to hip-hop potheads and then held it in with "Hits from the Bong," "I Want to Get High," and other blunt-inspired ditties.

❦ **17. "ROLL ANOTHER NUMBER (FOR THE ROAD)"** *Neil Young (1975)* Not too many people refer to joints as "numbers" anymore, but the stony sentiment expressed by a young Neil Young still holds true for anyone who knows they should head home at the end of a long night, but decides to roll up just one more anyway.

❦ **18. "SMOKE TWO JOINTS"** *Sublime (1992)* If Neil Young wanted to roll one more for the road (see above), leave it to the next generation to demand twice as much. In this cover of the Toyes original, super-stoners Sublime taught the world to double its pleasure with twice as much weed ("I smoke two joints in the morning / I smoke two joints at night / I smoke two joints in the afternoon, it makes me feel alright").

❦ **19. "DON'T STEP ON THE GRASS, SAM"** *Steppenwolf (1968)* Ever watch some stupid, hypocritical politician on TV talking about another victory in the War on Marijuana and just start yelling back at the screen? Well, Steppenwolf did you one better and wrote a song about it.

❦ **20. "PUFF THE MAGIC DRAGON"** *Peter, Paul & Mary (1963)* Three stoned-ass folkies from the '60s write a song about a magical dragon named Puff who takes you off to a mythical land of imagination. So is this kids' song *really* about marijuana? Does it matter?

Back in the day, album covers made perfect placemats for rolling joints.

THE BEST OF
BREWER & SHIPLEY
ONE TOKE OVER THE LINE

One Toke Over The Line • Tarkio Road • People Love Each Other
Fifty States Of Freedom • Shake Off The Demon • Have A Good Life
Witchi-Tai-To • Yankee Lady • All Along The Watchtower • Oh Mommy
Rise Up (Easy Rider) • Ruby On The Morning • The Light • Lady Like You

A CHILD'S GARDEN OF
GRASS
A PRE-LEGALIZATION COMEDY

WILLIE NELSON
COUNTRYMAN

Bob Marley and The Wailers
Catch A Fire

PETER TOSH

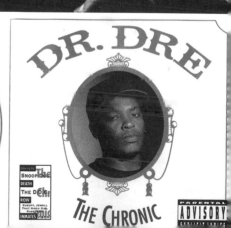

DR. DRE
THE CHRONIC

SNOOP
DEATH
ROW

PARENTAL
ADVISORY

HIGH TIMES ALL-STARS *The stoniest athletes in the doublewide world of sports*

In 2001, Toronto Raptors power forward Charles Oakley, a 17-year veteran of the NBA, observed that not only do 60 percent of professional basketball players smoke weed regularly, but "you got guys out there playing high every night."

So is cannabis a performance-enhancing drug? Smoking a joint certainly won't turn a klutz into a quarterback, but for some athletes, the marijuana high closely resembles "the zone" they enter at times of peak performance. It's also a great way to unwind after the game without the hangovers and indiscretions of alcohol. And as the following smoke-filled hall of fame proves, you needn't give up on natural grass if you want to win the big game.

NFL All-Pro tailback Ricky Williams runs through a field of nice dreams.

🌿 FOOTBALL

Mark Stepnoski The president of Texas NORML can kick your ass. At 6-foot-2 and 265 pounds, Mark Stepnoski was small to be a center in the NFL, but he's huge by stoner standards. After making five trips to the Pro Bowl and earning two Super Bowl rings, the Dallas Cowboy legend retired into a life of activism with the National Organization for the Reform of Marijuana Laws.

"I read *The Emperor Wears No Clothes* by Jack Herer about ten years ago, and I began reading *High Times*," Stepnoski explained to *HT* in a recent interview. "And the more I learned about the issue, the more I felt that marijuana prohibition was wrong."

Ricky Williams After leading the league in rushing in 2002, NFL All-Pro running back Ricky Williams walked away from football following a failed drug test, citing a determination to keep smoking marijuana among his main reasons for early retirement. He returned, briefly, before heading north to the greener pastures of the Canadian Football League.

Nate Newton The six-time Pro Bowl offensive lineman was arrested in 2001 when police pulled over a van he was riding in and discovered 213 pounds of pot stored in cardboard boxes in the back seat. Five weeks later, he got popped again, this time with 175 pounds of herb in the car.

Newton, who had retired a year earlier after fourteen seasons in the NFL, was convicted of possession with intent to distribute marijuana and sentenced to thirty months in federal prison.

❧ BASEBALL

Bill Lee Known to fans and foes alike as "The Spaceman," Bill Lee was a big-league outcast who touted Eastern philosophy, defended Maoist China, and claimed he sprinkled marijuana on his buckwheat pancakes in the morning—the THC thus making him impervious to bus fumes while jogging to work at Boston's Fenway Park. Late in his career, fans in Montreal threw him hash from the stands. He even partied with George W. Bush.

"Back in '73, we rolled a couple of doobies and smoked them together," Lee told the *Montreal Gazette* prior to the 2000 presidential election. "And I can tell you, he definitely inhaled."

Orlando Cepeda The original OC was baseball's rookie of the year in 1958 and the league's first unanimous MVP award winner in 1967. The son of Puerto Rico's most famous baseball player, Cepeda was a hard-hitting first baseman who put up Hall of Fame numbers, but was initially denied entry to those hallowed halls because of one tiny mistake: In 1975, he was arrested in the Miami airport after attempting to pick up a shipment containing 160 pounds of Puerto Rican pot.

Cepeda, who started smoking in the late '60s to treat the pain from ten knee operations, served almost a year in prison.

High Times Bonghitters Masters of the "infield high rule," the legendary *High Times* softball team takes the field as the tokin' terror of the New York publishing league. Since 1996, the Bonghitters have posted a 78–11–6 record, including unbeaten streaks of 29 and 21 games, and four separate undefeated seasons. Annually pitted against

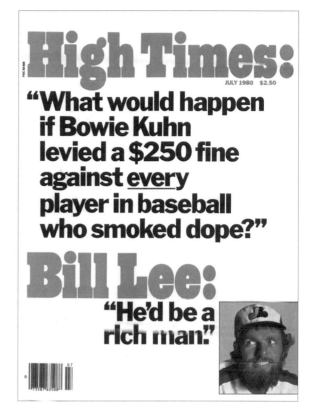

publications including *Playboy, Rolling Stone,* the *Onion,* the *New Yorker,* and archrivals the *Wall Street Journal,* our beloved Bonghitters rely on their trademark "rally joints" to inspire the team to new heights of hitting and fielding, while intimidating opponents into making errors whenever the sweet smell of natural grass wafts over from the stoned team's dugout.

Over the years, Bonghitter traditions have included a pregame Om circle, mascot Dreddy Duck throwing out the first pitch, and, at the conclusion of each contest, a team-wide rendition of "Take Me Out to the Bong Game," a serenade

that rings out across the great lawn of Manhattan's Central Park, followed by a classic three–part salute: *Hemp, hemp, HOORAY, Hemp, hemp, HOORAY, hemp, hemp, HOORAY!*

🌿 BASKETBALL

Kareem Abdul–Jabbar The NBA's career scoring leader (that's scoring buckets, not buds) got busted by U.S. Customs officials in 1998 at Pearson International Airport in Toronto, Canada, with six grams of marijuana. He was arrested again in 2001 after police pulled him over in Los Angeles. Jabbar apparently smokes pot to treat the severe migraine headaches that have plagued him since his playing days.

Robert Parish Also known as "The Chief," Boston Celtics center Robert Parish holds the record for most seasons played in the NBA (21) and most games played (1,611). So what's the secret of his longevity? Hard to say, but it's no secret he was arrested in 1991 after agents of the DEA intercepted a Federal Express package sent to his Massachusetts home that contained two ounces of pot.

Bill Walton Introducing the absolute worst person to have sitting in front of you at a Grateful Dead show: former NBA all–star, current TV commentator, and major deadhead Bill Walton. At 6–foot–11, you have no chance of seeing over him, and if he finds you during the set break and starts talking about help–side defense, you're in for a long night.

Walton, who saw dozens of Dead shows, including a private performance in front of the Egyptian pyramids in 1978, says he learned everything he really needed to know about playing hoops from Jerry and the boys: "They taught me the importance of delivering peak performances on demand, and to always play with a sense of joy and creativity," Walton says of the Dead. "They were just like a great basketball team . . . a group of outstanding individuals realizing that the strength of the team was the strength of the individual."

🌿 EXTREME SPORTS

Ross Rebagliati Winner of the men's giant slalom at the 1998 Winter Olympics, snowboarder Ross

Rebagliati briefly had his gold medal stripped from his chest after traces of THC were discovered in a post-race drug test. The medal was restored after an appeal by the Canadian Olympic Association.

Jen O'Brien & Bob Burnquist Could this be the world's most high-flying cannabis couple? O'Brien (a former *High Times* cover model) and Burnquist (a nominee for an ESPN Espy Award) both rank among the top skateboarders in the world.

"Pro boarding is such a go-go-go thing, and marijuana is the perfect way to wind down," Ms. O'Brien told *High Times*. "You can use it for inspiration as much as relaxation."

Z-Boys As old school as they come in the world of skateboarding, these punk kids from California defined a subgenre while still in their teens—surfing in the morning and skating in the afternoon, often after breaking into a backyard to borrow an empty swimming pool. Named for the Zephyr Competition Team that sponsored them in the seminal skate competitions of the '70s, the Boys grew rich and famous on wheels, and have since been the subject of both a Hollywood film (*Lords of Dogtown*) and a documentary (*Dogtown and Z-Boys*). Best of all, they've been burning from the very beginning.

"We mostly smoked only the shittiest weed back then. But I felt I skated better on pot. I'd skate for an hour or so, get in the groove, then take a little break and smoke a little," Z-boy Tony Alva told *High Times*. "Pot enhances the vibe, the perception. For me, that is."

BURNING BOOKS *The essential* High Times *library*

Sparking a spliff and starting off on the adventure of a new book can be one of the most rewarding pleasures in life. And just like marijuana, books can be mind-expanding substances, supplying you with not just a good read but also a new way to see the world. For example: An entire generation of hippies answered the call of their restless spirits after reading Jack Kerouac's *On the Road*, a tale of the endless search for the beatific through reefer, jazz, poetry, and free living in a time of crushing conformity. *The Electric Kool-Aid Acid Test* tells the tale of the stoned '60s flower children who picked up Kerouac's torch and took it all the way to the end of the road. And *Fear and Loathing in Las Vegas* serves up a bitter pill to swallow as the hippie highway reaches a seemingly dead end.

Naturally, not all of the titles included in our essential library have had the massive influence of *On the Road*, but they all have something stony to say and they all say it extremely well. Our ultimate *High Times* bookshelf includes fiction, nonfiction, gonzo journalism, how-to cultivation, and an autobiography, which means there's something for everyone, no matter what you like to read.

❦ **1. ON THE ROAD** *Jack Kerouac (1957)*
Ernest Hemingway once said that all American literature began with *Huckleberry Finn*, and if that's true it's also fair to say that all *hip* American literature began with *On the Road*, the story of shiftless, reefer-smoking beatniks Kerouac, Allen

Ginsberg, Neal Cassady, and the rest crisscrossing the country in search of girls, grass, good times, and an angelic understanding of authentic living amid the ruins of the American dream.

🌿 2. MARIJUANA HORTICULTURE *Jorge Cervantes (new edition, 2007)* Cannabis cultivators have been referring to this book as "The Bible" for over twenty-five years, and with good reason. Don't expect any divine intervention on behalf of your plants, but you will learn everything you ever

Ken Kesey and the Merry Pranksters took pot culture "Furthur" than ever before, with a little help from the original magic bus.

wanted to know about how to grow pot directly from the world's ultimate ganja guide. Full-color photos and easy-to-follow illustrations make this a must-have reference title for anyone growing reefer, and you can follow up every month in *High Times* with Jorge's question-and-answer column.

🌿 3. THE ELECTRIC KOOL-AID ACID TEST *Tom Wolfe (1968)* Much like his most famous protagonist, novelist Ken Kesey (*One Few Over the Cuckoo's Nest*) spent some serious time in a mental institution—albeit as a janitor, not an inmate. Through this odd job, he landed a part-time gig as a guinea pig in some of the earliest LSD experiments. After enjoying the acid experience, but not the experiments, the brazen young novelist stole a few samples from the lab, had them synthesized, and sparked a revolution, loading up the original psychedelic bus with LSD, marijuana, morning glory seeds, and anything else he could lay his hands on and taking off for the destination *Further* with Neal Cassady, thinly veiled hero of *On the Road*, behind the wheel.

When this hippie caravan returned home to the West Coast, Kesey held elaborate Acid Tests featuring spiked Kool-Aid, crazy light shows, and an unknown psychedelic house band called the Grateful Dead . . . and that's just the beginning of a true life story that's truly out of this world.

🌿 4. FEAR AND LOATHING IN LAS VEGAS *Hunter S. Thompson (1971)* The Godfather of gonzo journalism takes on hippies, hipsters, and squares alike in this drug-soaked satire of

American culture. Officially on assignment to cover a motor race in Las Vegas, things take a wrong, strange turn for our highly inebriated hero when he stumbles into the National District Attorney's Conference on Narcotics and Dangerous Drugs.

During his distinguished career, Hunter S. Thompson lent his good name and bad reputation to NORML to help end the persecution of potheads, and also appeared on the cover of *High Times* three times, including one of his last interviews in 2004, when he explained to our reporter why he loves to chat with the magazine.

"You're with *High Times*, right?" Hunter asked, right at the outset. "So you must have brought something good to smoke."

🌿 5. THE EMPEROR WEARS NO CLOTHES *Jack Herer (1985)* An underground publishing phenomenon, this "authoritative historical record of the cannabis plant, marijuana prohibition, and how hemp can still save the world" remains the seminal text of the modern hemp movement. Although Jack "The Hemperor" Herer may be best known these days for the super-potent cannabis strain that bears his name, well-rounded readers will still find astounding facts in this well-researched work of stoner scholarship. Just don't try to smoke the pages.

🌿 6. THE BEACH *Alex Garland (1996)* A young British backpacker in Thailand stumbles across a secluded beach on a restricted island, where a select few Westerners secretly live completely off the grid, fishing and gardening for food, sleeping under the stars, and wandering off into their neighbor's marijuana plantation whenever they need some buds. Sounds like a pothead's paradise, but can it last?

🌿 7. MR. NICE *Howard Marks (1996)* At one time connected with the British spy agency M16, the IRA, and the Mafia, Oxford-educated Howard Marks earned his nickname, and the title of his autobiography, by dealing huge shipments of cannabis with class and without violence, until the DEA finally caught up with him. In *Mr. Nice*, Marks spills the beans on a life spent moving pot and hash around the world, an astounding tale told by a true insider, with wit and charm to spare.

🌿 **8. DROP CITY** *T.C. Boyle (2003)* This brilliant novel centers around the "beautiful people" and easy living in a Northern California commune where idealism and reality meet face to face amid a pungent haze of pot smoke. Hardcore heads may prefer Boyle's novel *Budding Prospects*, about an ill-fated outdoor grow operation, but this is the superior story, particularly for anyone who ever wondered what it *really* must have been like to turn on, tune in, and drop out in the '60s.

🌿 **9. THE BOTANY OF DESIRE** *Michael Pollan (2002)* The gardening editor at the *New York Times Magazine*, Pollan tells the compelling life stories of four of our most common plants: apples, potatoes, tulips, and marijuana. Obviously, *High Times* subscribers will have the *Cannabis sativa* section "highlighted" for special consideration, but may we humbly suggest that you kindly consider reading all four entries, as you'll learn not only the long and winding tale of how high-grade marijuana came into existence, but also how all cultivated plants have shaped and reshaped themselves to satisfy mankind's desires, and how mankind has served those plants in kind.

🌿 **10. VINELAND** *Thomas Pynchon (1990)* Considered a solitary genius, and among America's top contemporary novelists, Pynchon may be best known for long and challenging epics like *Gravity's Rainbow* and *V.*, but here he turns his considerable talents to a highly readable evisceration of the War on Drugs by taking one of its victims and making him human. Zoyd Wheeler lives a quiet stoner life in Humbolt County, California, until one day a vindictive DEA man and a federally funded anti-marijuana operation turn his wife against him, and his life upside-down.

MARIJUANA AT THE MOVIES

Nothing beats getting stoned, settling in, and watching a movie (or two or three) on a rainy afternoon, whether you're hanging with your buddies, cuddling with your lover, or crashing out on the couch the day after a late night out on the town. Fortunately, some of the best films ever made make marijuana a central part of the plot, including comedies, dramas, and documentaries. Cannabis-loving cinephiles can also consider themselves blessed with an overwhelmingly wide selection of on-screen stoners to choose from, including outlaw bikers, Jamaican musicians, underwater explorers, self-deluded surfers, ganja-fueled super-geniuses, aging '60s radicals, partying '70s teenagers, and the average guy next door.

Hopefully, our list of the best stoner movies of all time will help you find the right film to suit your marijuana mood. Use only as directed, and make sure you have plenty of snacks on hand.

🌿 **1. EASY RIDER** *(1969)* Peter Fonda, Dennis Hopper, and Jack Nicholson all toked on real grass while filming this cannabis cult classic, including the legendary campfire scene where they introduced

OPPOSITE: *"Sure, we smoked marijuana on the picture." Jack Nicholson backs up fellow* Easy Rider *star Peter Fonda in the* National Enquirer, *1969.*

'I Smoke Marijuana Whenever I Feel Like It,' Says Peter Fonda

REAL THING: Fonda in a scene from the "Easy Rider" film in which he and two of his costars claim they were actually smoking marijuana.

FILM STAR Peter Fonda, 30, has a reputation for being a rebel.

By BILL SLOAN

"LSD gave me a whole new outlook on life," said rebellious young film star Peter Fonda. "Before I took it, I was highly depressed, nervous, agitated and paranoic.

"Until I took a 'trip' on LSD, I used to carry a loaded gun to protect myself from something I didn't even understand. But LSD eased my fears and had a lot of other positive results for me.

"LSD made me see that I had to do things, not think about them or hope about them," Fonda told this reporter in an exclusive interview. "I was 25 when I took my first LSD 'trip' and I found that I'd wasted those 25 years.

"For me, LSD was an interesting, positive experiment. I've also experimented with mescaline and other hallucinogenic drugs. And I smoke marijuana whenever I feel like it. Other people may have other reactions, but it just gives me a pleasant feeling. It makes me relax."

The 30-year-old Fonda, son of celebrated actor Henry Fonda and younger brother of Hollywood sex symbol Jane Fonda, admitted that his widely-acclaimed new film, "Easy Rider," is just one big "pot party" on the screen.

Fonda and his fellow actors, Jack Nicholson and Dennis Hopper, who, between them, wrote, directed, produced and starred in "Easy Rider," all admitted freely that they were smoking real marijuana in filmed scenes in the movie.

"Sure, we smoked marijuana in the picture," Nicholson confirmed to a reporter. "We were out in the country, and nobody was going to arrest us.

"It was a very insignificant thing and I didn't think much about it. Since I've been smoking it for 10 or 12 years, I have a fairly sophisticated point of view about it by now.

"I mean, everybody does it, don't they? Everybody I know does."

In another interview, Hopper talked freely about his own experiences with marijuana and remarked that 1969 is his 17th "grass-smoking year."

"Sure, print it, why not?" Hopper said. "You can say that was real pot we smoked in 'Easy Rider.' I've already been busted once for possession in L.A., but that's another story."

YOGA PUTS DOWN DOPE

Jeff Dowd, the real-life "Dude," makes quick work of his Lifetime Achievement Award trophy at the 2006 High Times Stony Awards.

Nicholson's character to marijuana for the first time. When the smoke cleared, this low-budget, high-concept tale of hippie bikers who were "born to be wild" had ignited an American independent cinema movement. *Easy Rider* also changed the way stoners could be depicted on the silver screen, replacing the usual homicidal maniacs with free-thinking, freewheeling revolutionaries. As Dennis Hopper explained in a *High Times* interview: "It was the first time anybody went out and smoked marijuana in a movie and didn't kill a whole bunch of nurses."

2. DAZED AND CONFUSED *(1993)*

Not much happens in this tale of stoned sub-urban youth, and yet everything happens. Set on the last day of school in 1976, the movie follows the inebriated exploits of a diverse group of students, including star quarterback Randall "Pink" Floyd, whose refusal to sign a pledge to the football team swearing off marijuana and his "loser friends" runs through the background of this often stony story. Set to a killer '70s soundtrack, *Dazed and Confused* brilliantly examines marijuana as a metaphor for freedom in a small Texas town where the football team represents a repressive mainstream culture that demands both your body and your soul.

3. THE BIG LEBOWSKI *(1998)* A box-

office disappointment when it first hit theaters, this twisted take on Hollywood's classic detec-tive yarns follows the exploits of The Dude, better known as Jeff Lebowski, an unemployed aging '60s radical who spends his days stoned and bowl-ing until a case of mistaken identity puts him back on the path of adventure. The movie may not have lasted long on the big screen, but couchlocked fans soon caught up once *The Big Lebowski* hit video, and today the cult of The Dude has grown so large that it supports an international series of Lebowksi Fests that draw thousands of "achievers" to revel in White Russians, doobies, Creedence, bowling, and all other things Lebowski, including a chance to meet Jeff Dowd, the real-life inspiration for the on-screen Dude.

"I've gotta be in shape to show up at a Lebowski Fest. I'm going to be challenged," Dowd explained

BEST POT SCENES

ANIMAL HOUSE *(1978)* Professor Pothead (a.k.a. Donald Sutherland) invites a few of his prized pupils to a very special session of "office hours" in the most popular college comedy of all time, locking the doors, shuttering the windows, and killing the lights before lighting up some grass and sparking a philosophical debate that ends with the timeless question: "Can I buy some pot from you?"

THE BREAKFAST CLUB *(1985)* What could finally bring together a princess, an athlete, a brain, a basketcase, and a criminal? How about a few fat doobies during detention? In this classic tale of teen angst overcome, the mismatched Breakfast Club find their common ground after fumigating the school library with pungent marijuana smoke. Then they dance like crazy.

ROMANCING THE STONE *(1984)* The "stone" in the title has nothing to do with marijuana, but this high-action adventure story does take a stony turn when Michael Douglas and Kathleen Turner find themselves stranded in the jungles of Colombia with a crashed plane filled with bales of marijuana. As night falls, they build a fire to stay warm . . . not to mention very, very happy.

SPECIAL ACHIEVEMENT AWARD—BEST STONER: SPICOLLI

FAST TIMES AT RIDGEMONT HIGH *(1982)* Sean Penn may be a major movie star and a radical political activist, but this perennial Oscar contender got his start as Jeff Spicolli, a struggling high school student who's a lot more interested in buds, babes, and waves than the finer points of American history. If you've only seen *Fast Times at Ridgemont High* on cable, get yourself an uncensored DVD and discover the truly stoner Spicolli within.

Hooray for Hollyweed.

to *High Times* after accepting a Lifetime Achievement trophy at our 2006 Stony Awards. "They all want to smoke their one best joint, or drink a double White Russian with The Dude, but I've gotta do it with forty of them—and still bowl."

4. UP IN SMOKE (1978)

Cheech & Chong's bud-dy act was already well-honed on stage by the time the dynamically stoned duo first brought their high-jinks to a major motion picture, a giant leap that made them household names even in households that *didn't* own a bong. They've since gone their separate ways, with Cheech Marin embracing mainstream films and TV, while Tommy Chong continues to revise his

pothead persona again and again, most famously in episodes of *That '70s Show* and in federal prison, where he served nine months in 2004 for selling marijuana paraphernalia.

Up in Smoke finds the world's most famous burnouts unwittingly driving a car literally made of marijuana across the border from Mexico, while trading some of the most famous one-liners of their storied career.

5. HALF BAKED (1998)

Dave Chappelle's first hit kept him high for a long time. Teamed up with Jim Brewer, Harland Williams, and Guillermo Diaz, Chappelle co-wrote *Half Baked* and starred as Thurgood, an enterprising custodian who steals medical marijuana from the lab where he works and sells it on the street to raise bail money for an incarcerated buddy. Some of the jokes may be a bit well-worn, but the movie has heart, soul, and a ton of weed smoking. Highlights include hilarious cameos from Jon Stewart (Enhancement Smoker), Willie Nelson (Historian Smoker), Tommy Chong (Squirrel Master), Snoop Dogg (Scavenger Smoker), Janeane Garofalo (I'm Only Creative When I Smoke Smoker), Stephen Baldwin (McGuyver Smoker), and Steven Wright as The Guy on the Couch.

6. THE LIFE AQUATIC WITH STEVE ZISSOU (2004)

Bill Murray was a 20-year-old premed student when he was caught trying to smuggle almost nine pounds of weed through O'Hare Airport in Chicago. The world may have lost a medicine man that day, but we gained one of our finest comedic actors. Murray has played notable stoners throughout his career, including a greenskeeper in *Caddyshack* who blends Kentucky Bluegrass and Northern California *Sinsemilla*, and his own personal friend Hunter S. Thompson in *Where the Buffalo Roam*. In *The Life Aquatic*, Murray finds himself cast as a struggling nature film director who enjoys smoking a little "seaweed" while producing his surreal underwater documentaries.

🌿 **7. FRIDAY** *(1995)* "I know you don't smoke weed; I know this, but I'm gonna get you high today, 'cause it's Friday; you ain't got no job . . . and you ain't got shit to do."

That's the promise Chris Tucker makes Ice Cube as this heavily blunted story opens in South Central Los Angeles. And it's a promise that Tucker, playing a low-level weed dealer named Smokey, has no trouble keeping, although his penchant for getting high on his own supply soon leads to serious trouble.

🌿 **8. HAROLD AND KUMAR GO TO WHITE CASTLE** *(2004)* The original title was "Harold and Kumar Get High as Fuck and Go to White Castle," which pretty much sums up the plot of this bud–laden buddy comedy. As Kal Penn (Kumar) explained to *High Times* in a 2004 interview: "I show up on the set at seven o'clock in the morning and I'm having a conversation with the producers and the director about how they're going to capture my character making love to a bag of weed. It was like, 'Okay, so Kal, we're going

Who knew that White Castle serves such happy meals?

to have you come over here and we'll have Weedie on the table and then we'll move to the bed.'" Weedie, of course, was the name of the giant bag of marijuana.

9. THE HARDER THEY COME *(1972)*

Jimmy Cliff's gritty examination of the highly corrupt Jamaican music scene portrays the struggle and desperation of a young reggae singer trying to make a name for himself, who finds that a life of dealing marijuana and street violence quickly brings him more money, fame, and respect than his stalled songwriting career. *The Harder They Come* introduced worldwide audiences to reggae music and Jamaican culture, offering a sobering look at life on the mean streets of Kingston a year before Bob Marley & the Wailers would release their breakthrough album *Catch a Fire*.

10. JAY AND SILENT BOB STRIKE BACK *(2001)*

In the ever inward-facing world of director Kevin Smith, superstoners Jay and Silent Bob take center stage in this *Clerks* sequel, which finds the mismatched partners in crime heading for Hollywood to stop an ill-fated movie adaptation of *Bluntman and Chronic*, a comic based on their imagined lives as the infamous "Doobage Duo," a pair of average potheads who decide to remake themselves as marijuana superheroes after winning the lottery. To make things even more confusing, an actual comic called *Bluntman and Chronic* was also produced in real life, based on the fictitious version that first appeared in the plot to Smith's earlier film *Chasing Amy*. Confused? Good—now go take a few dozen bong hits, and then you'll be ready to begin the journey . . .

11. AMERICAN BEAUTY *(1999)*

You don't get old (and lame) until you stop smoking pot. That's the stoner subtext in this ponderous, Academy Award–winning tale of a suburban dad who finds life losing all meaning as the mundane world of wife and kids chokes the last remnants of cool out of his system. The antidote: Find the dealer next door, score an ounce of the latest super-strain of marijuana, and start puffing away in the garage when nobody's looking. Kevin Spacey's character may get a little, well, *spacey*, not to mention erratic, but at least he feels alive again.

12. WOODSTOCK *(1970)*

If you were born too late for the Age of Aquarius, this beautiful, sprawling concert film may be the best way to relive the high spirits of the '60s without risking a trip to Vietnam. Inventively spliced together using a series of split screens, *Woodstock* offers up a sense of psychedelic overload, not to mention a front-row seat for the music festival that defined a generation, including the tokers, the trippers, and the victims of the brown acid. Highlights include musical performances from the biggest (and baked-est) names in classic rock, featuring Crosby, Stills & Nash; The Who; Joe Cocker; Jimi Hendrix; Santana; and Sly & the Family Stone performing their latest hit, "I Want to Take You Higher."

13. FEAR AND LOATHING IN LAS VEGAS *(1998)*

Johnny Depp logged some serious time at author Hunter S. Thompson's legendary "fortified compound" in Woody Creek, Colorado, before attempting to bring the infamously drug-crazed writer to life in the film adaptation of Hunter's most famous bit of gonzo journalism (see "Burning Books," page 83). *Fear and Loathing in Las Vegas* takes you deep inside one of the sharpest and most altered minds in American letters for "a savage journey to the heart of the American dream."

❧ **14. HOW HIGH** *(2001)* Method Man and Redman got their start on the mean streets of Staten Island, running and rapping with the legendary Wu-Tang Clan, a shaolin-inspired crew that represents East Coast heads with blunt-inspired beats and rhymes. *How High* finds Meth and Red taking a Cheech & Chong turn as lowbrow guys vaulted into higher education after cultivating a super-strain of Mary Jane that increases your IQ with every puff. Next stop: Harvard.

❧ **15. TRAILER PARK BOYS: THE MOVIE** *(2006)* Alert the Border Patrol, Homeland Security, and the DEA: Canada's homegrown heroes have arrived in America with the release of *Trailer Park Boys: The Movie*, a feature film based on their JUNO Award–winning television show. Already a mainstream hit north of the border, the infamously foul-mouthed mockumentary follows the always illicit adventures of the denizens of Sunnyvale Trailer Park, a loveable bunch of cannabis-cultivating, hash-hockey-playing, gun-wielding, grill-stealing, porn-filming, bootlegging best friends who somehow manage to spend the majority of their off-camera time in prison.

❧ **16. GRASS** *(1999)* Director Ron Mann's powerful documentary film examines the history

Canada's homegrown heroes, the Trailer Park Boys, enjoy some high times in their legendary shitmobile.

of the marijuana laws, revealing the racism, fear-mongering, and social control at the root of cannabis prohibition, and then taking a chronological approach to recounting our illogical War on Chronic. Marijuana activist Woody Harrelson lent his voice as narrator free of charge, telling the long, sordid story of anti-pot propaganda while over four hundred hours of compiled archival footage gets ably edited down to a highly enlightening eighty-seven minutes.

*Best buds Jack Black and Kyle Gass join forces
to form Tenacious D.*

a brilliant album of "acoustic metal," toured the country several times, made the cover of *High Times,* and finally filmed their first movie, a chronicling of their journey from open mic nights to superstardom, with plenty of tasty bong hits along the way.

 Tenacious D has always stood firmly behind the herb, performing at NORML benefits and declaring in their song "City Hall" that, once they rule the world as two kings, their first act will be to legalize marijuana. As Jack Black decrees: "The tyranny, and the bullshit, have gone on too long."

🌿 17. TENACIOUS D IN THE PICK OF DESTINY (2006)

Before Jack Black became a major Hollywood star, he was best known as the smaller half of Tenacious D, self-described greatest band on Earth, and an instant cult classic once their short films started airing on HBO in 1999. The D subsequently left pay cable, recorded

🌿 18. SUPER TROOPERS (2001)

What if the cops had a sense of humor? In *Super Troopers,* a group of Vermont state troopers stuck in a small town spend more time playing pranks on each other than actually fighting crime. Police work takes a backseat to high-jinks until the troopers find themselves tasked with busting up an herb-smuggling ring moving weight across the Canadian border.

🌿 19. JORGE CERVANTES' ULTIMATE GROW (2005)

High Times presents this best-selling series of instructional DVDs from Jorge Cervantes, author of *Marijuana Horticulture* and the world's most trusted ganja guide. The first installment covers all the basics for beginners, taking you from seed to harvest in high style, while *Ultimate Grow 2* follows Jorge to his home country of Spain, and includes indoor, outdoor, greenhouses, hydro, organic, and even a guerrilla garden hidden in the Spanish countryside.

🌿 **20.** *Double Feature:* **REEFER MADNESS** *(1936) and* **HEMP FOR VICTORY** *(1942)*

Anti-pot propaganda just doesn't get any better than *Reefer Madness*, a church-backed "educational" film that helped spawn pot prohibition by depicting a world in which one puff leads to instant insanity. You'll laugh so hard it will hurt, especially when you consider that these awful misconceptions still plague us today, along with the misguided laws they helped get on the books. Better watch *Hemp for Victory!* right afterward, and let the U.S. Department of Agriculture's World War II–era plea for increased hemp farming to help the war effort convince you that the federal government can't be *all* bad.

RASTAMAN VIBRATIONS

In the 1930s, a new religious movement sprang up among the working class and poor in Jamaica, focused on Haile Selassie I, then the emperor of Ethiopia. Believing Selassie to be Jah, God incarnate on Earth, as foretold in the prophecies of both the Old and New Testaments, the Rastafarian faith evolved throughout the 20th century into a complex blend of Judeo-Christian and Afrocentric religious beliefs, deeply influenced by the movement's Caribbean roots. To outsiders, Rastas remain best known for their ganja, dreadlocks, and reggae music, particularly Bob Marley, who spread not only reggae but Rasta across the globe, including making a pilgrimage to Ethiopia a few years before his untimely death. Today, up to 10 percent

Damian Marley, a second-generation Rastafarian, enjoys a little ganja and some light reading backstage at the Bonnaroo music festival.

of Jamaicans identify themselves as Rastafarians, with millions more followers all over the world.

Not all Rastas get high, but the movement as a whole enthusiastically praises the herb as a cleansing sacrament and a means of communing with Jah. Alcohol, which is forbidden, is associated with violence, exploitation, and wickedness, while ganja brings peace, insight, and righteousness.

THE FUNNY PAPERS

"Grass will carry you through times of no money better than money will carry you through times of no grass," according to Freewheelin' Franklin, the sharpest head among the Fabulous Furry Freak Brothers—three stoned-out roommates who brought the world of underground comix to new heights of hilarity in the 1970s, including a long run as the house strip in *High Times* magazine. Marijuana appeared in and inspired the work of many founding fathers of underground comix, including R. Crumb, creator of the hard-partying Fritz the Cat and guru-icon Mr. Natural.

Today, there's little difference between comics and comix—both are big business—and the underground appeal of pot smoking still finds a home in the art form, including daily comic strips like "The Boondocks," which had this to say after President George W. Bush got caught on tape admitting to youthful marijuana smoking: "Bush got recorded admitting that he smoked weed. . . . Maybe he smoked it to take the edge off the coke." That strip was censored by the *Chicago Tribune*,

prompting Boondocks creator Aaron McGruder to add "marijuana activist" to his long list of progressive political causes.

HIGH SOCIETY *Choice quotes from the* High Times *interview archives*

Not every pot-smoking celebrity has the guts to talk to *High Times*. We only get the ones who really love the plant and want *everyone* to know. Still, over the past three decades, some of the biggest and coolest names in music, movies, literature, pot, and politics have sat down for a sesh with our reporters, and given the unique headspace most of these conversations take place within, you just never know what's going to get said in a *High Times* interview.

🌿 **JOHN WATERS** *(1983)* "No matter how much I liked it, I could never say to someone, 'I'd like some Maui Wowie,' I would be so mortified to say that to someone. The high could never compensate."

🌿 **ROB THOMAS** *(2005)* "When I travel, I'll buy a $10 bong and then ditch it or give it to a friend. At home, I have a plastic one and a two-foot glass one that someone got me for Christmas, but I don't use the big one too much. It's like the good china you bring out when company comes over."

🌿 **SEAN PAUL** *(2006)* "A pothead is a lot different than a wino or a crackhead. A pothead is a considerate person who thinks about life and the people around him."

MICK JAGGER (1979) "I know what people spend on drugs. You've got to look it up in *High Times*. It's a fortune. Grass is a hundred dollars an ounce—a hundred and fifty dollars for an ounce of grass. It's unbelievable."

STEPHEN KING (1981) "I think that marijuana should not only be legal, I think it should be a cottage industry. It would be wonderful for the state of Maine. There's some pretty good homegrown dope. . . . What we've got up there are lobsters, potatoes, and a lot of poor people. My wife says, and I agree with her, that what would be really great for Maine would be to legalize dope completely and set up dope stores the way that there are state-run liquor stores. You could get your Acapulco Gold or your whatever it happened to be—your Augusta Gold or your Bangor Gold. And people would come from all the other states to buy it, and there could be a state tax on it. Then everybody in Maine could have a Cadillac."

TREY ANASTASIO (2002) "I should probably smoke more pot when I'm recording an album. You sit in the studio for four hours staring at a soundboard, and then you start to lose perspective. Smoking pot is a way of changing perspective."

BOB MARLEY (1976) "It's time to let de people get good herbs an' smoke. Government's a joke. All dey wan' is ya smoke cigarettes and cigar. . . . Some big cigar me see man wit', me tell him must smoke herb. Me wanna see a nice level piece of green grass."

NORMAN MAILER (2004) "I was out in the car listening to the radio. Some jazz came on. I'd been listening to jazz for years, but it had never meant all that much to me. Now, with the powers pot offered, simple things became complex; complex things clarified themselves. These musicians were offering the inner content of their experiences to me."

CHEECH MARIN (1976) "Even when you could get the death penalty for smoking, I used to smoke, and practically the same amount that I do now."

NOAM CHOMSKY (1988) "One of the traditional and obvious ways of controlling people in every society, whether it's a military dictatorship or a democracy, is to frighten them. If people are frightened, they'll be willing to cede authority to their superiors who will protect them. . . . The Drug War is an effort to stimulate fear of dangerous people from whom we have to protect ourselves. It is also a direct form of control of what are called the 'dangerous classes,' those superfluous people who don't really have a function contributing to profit-making and wealth. They have to be somehow taken care of."

SUSAN SONTAG (1978) "I think marijuana is much better than liquor. I think a society which is addicted to a very destructive and unhealthy drug—namely alcohol—certainly has no right to complain or be sanctimonious or censor the use of a drug which is much less harmful."

August 1980 $2.50

HIGHTIMES

Will success spoil Cheech & Chong? Of course. See page 32.

High Times

August '77

$1.75

COCA-COLA AND COCAINE
The Pause
That Refreshes

THE LOLITA COMPLEX
Titties, Tushies & Teddy Bears

Is There a
KILLER NARC SQUAD?
Col. Lucien Conein
Has the Answer

DOLLY PARTON
Lets Her Hair Down

THE GREAT
GRASS TRIALS
Starring
Robert Mitchum
and Candy Barr

THE FURRY
FREAK BROS.
Visit the Outlaw
Rock Festival

Murder at Elaine's
Part 3

INTERVIEW WITH
ANDY WARHOL:
CAMPBELL'S SOUP,
PAPER DOLLS
AND THE DEATH
OF ART

Coca-Cola

🍁 **JIMMY BUFFETT** *(1976)* "I don't get stoned before shows, but afterwards I get real high . . ."

🍁 **ABBIE HOFFMAN** *(1980)* "I'm innocent. Completely innocent. *Crime* is one of the most complicated words to define. One person's crime is another person's means of survival. The prose-cutor asked for $500,000 bail in my case as he adjusted his tie for the newspaper boys. He said, and I quote, 'This is a crime more heinous than murder.' That was six years ago. Now, the prose-cutor, that same guy, is a partner in a dope case with one of my lawyers; he goes into court and claims coke is harmless. He gets clients off. He's a good lawyer. So who's on first?"

🍁 **ALI G** *(2003)* "Me can roll up two spliffs using one hand—dat iz why I iz known as bein' double-jointed, *a'ight*?"

🍁 **ANI DIFRANCO** *(2004)* "If I use just the right amount of cannabis, at just the right time, it can be incredibly instructive. It makes me drop my preconceptions about what I'm doing—all of the subliminal mental stuff that has to do with the babble of society. It makes me experience music viscerally and very spiritually."

🍁 **DAVE CHAPPELLE** *(2004)* "When I think about the people I have smoked pot with, they're such an eclectic mix of people, and I probably never would have spoken to a lot of them if it weren't for pot. Alcohol doesn't bring people together like that."

TOP: *Hey Dave Chappelle, what's that behind your ear?*
ABOVE: *When we asked why he posed for the cover of* High Times, *Ali G responded: "Coz u iz de only mag dat pay in weed."*

Willie Nelson knows that it's NORML to smoke pot.

🌿 **THE GAME** *(2005)* "Amsterdam was like weed heaven. I felt like Noah—I could've built me an ark out of weed. I almost cried when we had to leave. I was looking out the bus window and waving like in one of those movies."

🌿 **WILLIE NELSON** *(2005)* "I knew I was killing myself with cigarettes, and I knew I was really putting myself in danger with drinking so much. . . . In the early years I drank all the time. Before pot."

🌿 **KEITH RICHARDS** *(1978)* "There's all this flimflam about decriminalization, which isn't legalization, and eventually what it comes down to is money anyway. If they can figure out a way of taking it over and making bread out of it, it'll be legal. . . . Let's just say that I can't see myself, or anybody that I know, preferring to buy a pack of prerolled marijuana cigarettes when I know that it's going to be Grade C."

🌿 **SNOOP DOGG** *(2000)* "If the government legalized weed, the crime rate would go down. People would just wanna chill."

🌿 **T.C. BOYLE** *(1999)* "You know what the government makes off a pack of cigarettes, a gallon of gasoline, or a bottle of booze? We could do the same with pot and hash."

🌿 **ANDY WARHOL** *(1977)* *High Times:* "Do you ever smoke pot?"

Andy Warhol: "No, but I like the smell of it."

MAXIMIZE THE POWER OF PA

HIGH TIMES

JUL 323

CELEBRATING THE COUNTERCULTURE

SNOOP DOGG
STONER OF THE YEAR

3RD STONY AWARDS

12 GROW GUIDE

ARREN AYNES

UDDLE F MUDD

OLLYWOOD

07>

JULY 2002

$4.99
$5.99

48427

420
THINGS TO
DO WHEN
YOU'RE
STONED

Every year on April 20, the *High Times* phone lines start ringing off the hook. Some of the calls come from our 420-friendly friends, wanting to wish us a happy 4/20 (the official high holiday of potheads all across the world), but most of the inquiries arrive via the mainstream media, a group of clueless non-tokers still wondering how it all got started. They know by now that 420 serves as a secret stoner code, but they have no idea what to make of it.

As we patiently explain, 420 is not police code for marijuana smoking in progress, it's not the number of molecules in cannabis, and no, it's not the official time to serve "high tea" in polite British society. Learn your highstory, and you'll know the tradition originated with a group of students in San Rafael, California, who met at 4:20 every afternoon to share the sacred sacrament (see page 22). The good news is that what started as underground slang has now reached the marijuana masses, giving us a universal and semi-discreet way to self-identify, but the bad news is that the word has gotten out so far that the straight world has cracked our code.

So what's the best way to celebrate 420, now that it's out in the open? Getting really, really baked, of course, but what next? You should find plenty of inspiration in the comprehensive list below . . . or feel free to send us your own suggestions (420highdeas@hightimes .com). We're always looking for new ways to enjoy getting high.

1 JOIN NORML
What's NORML? According to the National Organization for the Reform of Marijuana Laws, it's normal to smoke pot. NORML is also the oldest and largest organization dedicated solely to securing the rights of marijuana smokers—i.e., you—and there's no better time to join than now, while you're nice and stoned. For more info, visit www.norml.org.

2 PLAY BADMINTON

3 TRAVEL THE GLOBE
There's no better way to see the world than through a pair of red eyes, whether your journey takes you to the Rif Mountains in Morocco or just the other end of town.

4 GO BAREFOOT

5 MEDITATE

6 LEARN TO ROLL
Roll a stoner a joint, and he gets high today; teach a stoner to roll, and he gets high forever.

7 TAKE A HIKE

8 ROCK OUT
The connection between music and marijuana is as old as herb itself. When *High Times* asked Grammy Award–winner Damian Marley if ganja was part of his creative process, he told us sagely, "It's part of my *every* process."

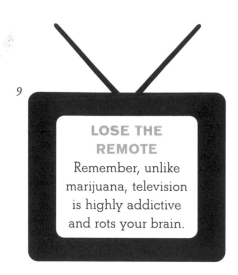

9

LOSE THE REMOTE

Remember, unlike marijuana, television is highly addictive and rots your brain.

10 **DEMAND A RAISE**

11 **GO SEE A LOCAL BAND**

12 **HELP A FRIEND OUT OF A JAM**

13 **WRITE A LETTER TO THE EDITOR**

14 **SAVE THE PLANET**

15 **PLANT A GARDEN**

We're thinking about vegetables at the moment, but if you'd rather harvest some nice "herbs," kindly check out "Where Does Marijuana Come From?" (page 177) for a few tips on acquiring a green thumb.

16 **CLEAN YOUR BONG**

If the water in the bottom is both the color and consistency of chocolate pudding, it's definitely high time for a little scrubbing . . . then you can get stoned all over again.

17 **FLY A KITE**

Extra points if you happen to (re)discover electricity while you're at it . . .

18 **RIDE A BICYCLE**

They're fun, good exercise, and save fossil fuels.

19 **SHAKE YOUR ((BOOTY))**

20 **BAKE WHILE YOU'RE BAKED**

21 **RENT A MOVIE**

22 **MAKE A MOVIE**

23 **MAKE A NEW FRIEND**

You might start by sharing the rest of that joint.

24 **CALL AN OLD FRIEND**

CELEBRITY HIT – REDMAN

25 **WORK**

"When I smoke, it's not a downer for me. I don't want to just eat chips and watch TV and shit. I want to create. I might write rhymes for a couple of hours, then try to go do a beat for a couple of hours, then engineer one of my homies' shit, learning Pro Tools for a couple of hours, then I'm back writing. Everyone smokes a lot in my studio, but we don't sit around."

26 **TRY YOGA**

Just don't smoke too much before attempting to tuck your feet behind your head . . .

27 **BUILD A FORT**

Once it's built you'll have a great new place to smoke weed.

28 TURN A CARTWHEEL
Been a while, hasn't it?

29 FEED THE CAT
You're both hungry, but the cat can't feed herself. Oh, and a little catnip is always appreciated as well.

30 DIG A HOLE TO CHINA

31 CARVE A JACK-O'-LANTERN
Admittedly, this is most popular right before Halloween, but then again, why wait?

32 HIDE SOME WEED
Put a joint somewhere you won't find it for a week or so . . . you'll thank us later.

33 DO IT YOURSELF

34 STOP STRESSING

35 TRY JUGGLING
Might want to start with something a little easier than flaming chainsaws, though . . .

36 DOODLE
Bonus points: Make a little flipbook on the edge of a stack of Post-it Notes.

37 BURN SOME INCENSE
Just don't expect it to disguise your smoky smells. Everybody knows about incense . . .

38 SING A SONG TO YOUR SWEETHEART

39 STUDY KARATE

40 ACT IN A PLAY

41 GO CAMPING
How do you think 'smores were invented, anyway?

42 HACKYSACK
A bit cliché perhaps, but it's a lot more fun than kicking around a bowling ball.

43 GAZE AT THE STARS
Take a nice big toke, squint a little, and the Big Dipper looks a lot like a pipe.

44 LAUGH OUT LOUD
Odds are something's funny. If not, you may need to smoke a bit more . . .

45 PRACTICE YOUR CHEECH & CHONG IMITATIONS
Dave's not here, man . . .

46 SMILE

47 SUMO WRESTLE

48 STUDY PERMACULTURE

49 MAKE LOVE
Whoever said that power is the ultimate aphrodisiac never smoked really good weed.

50 COUNT YOUR BLESSINGS

51 MASTURBATE

52 PLAY SCRABBLE

53 GO BIRDWATCHING

54 SNOWBOARD AT DAWN

55 DO YOUR LAUNDRY

56 FIGHT CITY HALL

57 TIE YOUR SHOES

58 OVERCOME YOUR PREJUDICES

59 CROSS A CULTURAL DIVIDE

60 TAKE A WALK

61 GET A MASSAGE

62 GIVE A MASSAGE

63 QUIT YOUR JOB

64 SING IN THE SHOWER

65 SHOOT SOME POOL

66 FLIRT

67 DO YOUR NAILS

68 START A SNOWBALL FIGHT

69 RIDE A ROLLER COASTER

70 BEG FORGIVENESS

71 SKATEBOARD WHERE IT'S NOT PERMITTED

72 HAVE A GOOD CRY
It's not only cleansing, it also gives you a good alibi for having red eyes.

73 WATCH THE CLOUDS GO BY
Yes, we know—that one in the middle definitely looks just like Jerry Garcia.

74 TERRORIZE AN ALL-YOU-CAN EAT RESTAURANT

75 WRITE TO CONGRESS
Tell those bastards in Washington, D.C., to stop arresting marijuana smokers—just don't call them bastards, at least not to their faces.

STAFF PICK – NATASHA (MANAGING EDITOR)
76 GO TO THE GYM
"I'm going to get the munchies anyway, so I like to launch a preemptive strike on my thighs. Plus, I psych myself into thinking I can lift more, run faster, and Jazzercise with greater panache."

77 GET MARRIED
Scientific studies prove that cannabis couples have more fun, stay together longer, and always finish their slices of wedding cake.

78 LIVE THE LIFE YOU'VE IMAGINED

79 FIGHT THE POWERS THAT BE

80 LEARN TO SEW

81 LOVE THY NEIGHBOR

82 SWIM UPSTREAM
Literally or figuratively, or both at the same time if you can pull it off without drowning.

83 WHISTLE A CATCHY TUNE

84 COOK DINNER
You may not be hungry at the moment, but you will be in about ten minutes—trust us—and no amount of store-bought munchies can satisfy a stoner like a home-cooked meal.

85 SOLVE A MYSTERY

86 CALL MOM
She'll be so happy to hear from you, and over the phone there's no way she can tell you're stoned—plus, there might be some cookies in it the next time you see her!

87 RUN AWAY AND JOIN THE CIRCUS

88 BUILD A SWEAT LODGE

89 HAVE A THREESOME

90 STOP AND SMELL THE ROSES

91 MAKE SPIN ART
Okay, it never looks quite as cool once it stops spinning, so just let the motherfucker keep on turning and pack another bong . . .

92 HOST A GARAGE SALE
Join the anarchistic economy of untaxed, unregulated commerce; earn extra money for herb; and get rid of some old junk all at the same time . . . *Hey man, that spin art is not for sale!*

93 Defy Expectations

94 READ A BOOK
Yes, you're reading a book right now, and yes, you're stoned, but there's a lot more great reads out there waiting. Check out "Burning Books" (page 83) if you need a recommendation.

95 WRITE A BOOK
Try something with a snazzy title like *The Official* High Times *Pot Smoker's Handbook*—actually, that one might be taken . . .

96 TAKE A SIESTA

97 PLAY MATCHMAKER

98 DOWNLOAD YOUR FAVORITE BAND'S FIRST ALBUM

99 SYNC UP *DARK SIDE OF THE MOON* AND *THE WIZARD OF OZ*

100 SURRENDER TO FATE

101 COMFORT A FRIEND

102 FIX YOUR CAR

103 RAKE THE LAWN

104 FIND A NEW APARTMENT

105 RESOLVE A DISPUTE
Hey, they don't call it the "peace pipe" for nothing.

106 FLOSS

107 WIN AN ARGUMENT

108 PLAN A PICNIC

109 CLEAN OUT THE GARAGE

STAFF PICK – ELISE (PRODUCTION DIRECTOR)
110 CRUISE FOR COOL TRASH
"Back in the day, my girlfriends and I would roll up a phatty, puff down, and then cruise wealthy neighborhoods on trash day. Sometimes we discovered the most amazing stuff . . . dart boards, paintings, aquariums . . . and on one cloudy morning, an awesome green velvet couch that still sits in my living room to this day!"

111 LOOK THROUGH OLD PHOTO ALBUMS

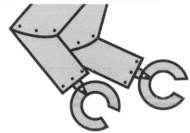

STAFF PICK – CRAIG (DIRECTOR OF TECHNOLOGY)
"I challenge anyone to play 18 hours of continuous EverQuest without weed."

First on the list: Stop coughing . . . okay, seriously, you may not always feel like doing something productive while stoned, but it can actually be a great time to get highly organized.

This can be wonderful or horrible depending upon the severity of your munchies and what you've got lying around the fridge. Note: Pickles and ketchup are not good in a milkshake—trust us, we've tried.

ACTIVIST PICK — ALLEN ST. PIERRE (NORML'S HEAD HONCHO)
157 **GO FLY FISHING**

"Fly fishermen love to wax poetic about their many weeks and months spent concentrating on a particular body of water, typically a small trout stream; their hours spent communing with nature and making painstaking observations—from dawn to dusk—of the feeding habits and patterns of their chosen quarry. But I work 60 to 70 hours a week on marijuana law reform in a large megalopolis far from any trout stream, so how can I distill the many hours needed to commune with nature and observe the ways of the trout down to its bare essence?

For me, the answer is to imbibe cannabis. By incorporating some high-quality ganja or hash into my fishing forays, I find myself more quickly relating to nature, sharpening my powers of observation, and, frankly speaking, becoming one with the trout. I'd surely enjoy an extended holiday for fishing and plying remote waterways, but absent such an opportunity, my use of cannabis in conjunction with fly-fishing is a dearly held mode of deep relaxation and creates a profound sense of oneness with my natural surroundings."

STAFF PICK – NICO ESCONDIDO (CULTIVATION REPORTER)
162 **CALL 4-2-0 ON A FUCKING COP**
"First, I like to get stoned—really baked, with red eyes and all . . . then I eat a whole lot of colored jellybeans and drink as much milk as I can. I then walk into a police station asking for a Medicinal Cannabis Clinic. At that point, I explain marijuana calms my stomach and that I feel sick. Then, amidst the laughter, when no one is looking, I stick my finger down my throat and barf all over the station."

Just don't try to smoke the centerfold.

SPIN AROUND IN CIRCLES UNTIL YOU'RE DIZZY

181 LEARN AN INSTRUMENT
Can't make music until you know how to play, unless, of course, you're in a punk band . . .

182 PLAY BACKGAMMON

183 WRITE A STONER COMEDY MOVIE SCRIPT

184 FIND A FOUR-LEAF CLOVER

185 GO TRICK–OR–TREATING

186 EXPERIENCE A LUNAR ECLIPSE

187 SCUBA DIVE

188 SWIM WITH DOLPHINS

189 WATCH THE SUPER BOWL
While you smoke a super bowl . . .

190 CONNECT THE DOTS

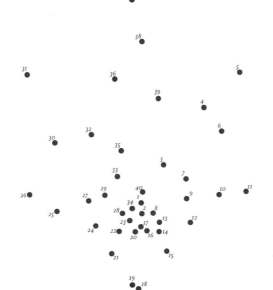

STAFF PICK – DANNY DANKO (CULTIVATION EDITOR)
191 TEND TO MY PLANTS
"A nice electric *sativa* buzz is perfect for ganja gardening. Qualities such as increased concentration and intense patience ensure that each individual plant gets the attention it needs. Plants will reward you later for your due diligence now."

192 SKYDIVE

193 SWIM BENEATH A WATERFALL

194 KEEP A JOURNAL
There's no better way to remember all that stuff that keeps happening to you, especially if your short-term memory just ain't what it used to be . . .

195 TALK LIKE A BEATNIK

196 HEAD FOR MARDI GRAS

197 MAKE YOUR OWN WEB SITE

198 BARTEND A PARTY

199 VISIT THE PYRAMIDS

200 GO BUNGEE JUMPING

201 PLAY AIR GUITAR
No time to learn an instrument? No problem. Just don't expect many groupies.

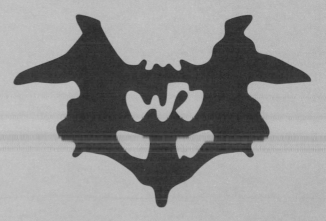

STAFF PICK – STEVEN HAGER (EDITOR IN CHIEF)
"My favorite thing to do while getting high is to watch a glorious sunset. In December, this daily event takes place around 4:20 p.m., which makes for an extra-special holiday experience."

MAKE YOUR OWN GUACAMOLE

Get off the couch, find the leash, and take Fido for a spin around the neighborhood. You'll both feel a lot better out in the fresh air, especially the dog.

328 BUILD A GRAVITY BONG
(see page 48)

329 ACE YOUR JOB INTERVIEW
Warning: Works best if you're interviewing for a job at *High Times*.

330 PHILOSOPHIZE

331 FANTASIZE ABOUT SOMETHING FORBIDDEN

332 BOWL
Fuck it dude, let's go bowling . . .

333 GET LOST

334 GET FOUND

335 FINISH YOUR MANIFESTO

336 TELL GHOST STORIES

337 VISIT A MAYAN RUIN

338 WANDER THE DESERT

339 Read The Newspaper

Just make sure you keep your bullshit detectors fully engaged.

340 LISTEN TO THE RAIN HIT THE ROOF

341 SCRAPE YOUR PIPE FOR RESIN

342 REDECORATE YOUR BEDROOM

343 RIDE A UNICYCLE

ACTIVIST PICK – KEITH STROUP (NORML'S FOUNDER)
344 COOK A MEAL
"I love to do some serious cooking when I'm stoned. For me, there are few things I enjoy more than planning a good meal, shopping for the fresh ingredients, and working through the various steps of preparation and cooking—generally slow cooking—the food. Of course, I keep my cookbooks readily available during the several hours this entails, as short-term memory loss occasionally requires me to reread the recipes more than once. . . . The final reward is the opportunity to fully enjoy the meal and appreciate the subtle tastes involved, while sharing the experience with someone you love."

345 GO TO BINGO NIGHT

346 SEE A SYMPHONY ORCHESTRA
Better leave those glowsticks at home . . .

347 CHANGE YOUR PLANS

348 SEIZE THE DAY

349 IMPEACH THE PRESIDENT

350 DANCE IN A STROBE LIGHT

351 PLAY SOME FOOSBALL

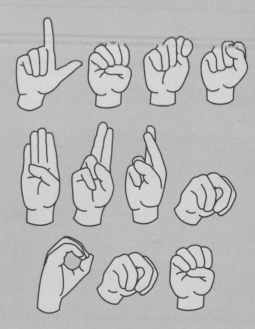

394 EXPAND YOUR HORIZONS

GANJA GLOBETREKKING

Pack your bags (and your bongs) for a THC-laden trek across the globe. From Amsterdam's infamous coffeeshops to the massive fields in Morocco that provide those shops with their finest hashish, it's definitely a small, green, well-connected world when it comes to cannabis. And while nowhere on Earth can currently match the freedom afforded to our kind in the Netherlands, countless other locations and events also cater to adventurous herbalists who know that, when it comes to traveling, getting stoned is half the fun.

Ever ask God to send you a sign?

If your ideal vision of a ganja getaway brings to mind reggae music, white sand beaches, and bright green *sativas* sold by the handful, you'll find *irie* times and plenty of *kaya* to smoke in Jamaica, *mon*. Or perhaps you'd prefer puffing ornamental hookahs stuffed full of aromatic hashish in a centuries-old Nepalese bazaar. Or maybe getting high on vacation means smoking a spliff of BC bud on the chairlift at Whistler Mountain in Vancouver, British Columbia, home to both the 2010 Winter Olympics and some of the finest Maple Leaf marijuana Canada has to offer. Or you could hit the famous backpacker's trail in

Thailand, and find out if they still have Thai stick. Or stay stateside and *make* money for your next journey by finding work in Northern California during harvest season . . .

But remember, as always, smoke with your head, not over it. Believe it or not, some places in the world have stricter laws against marijuana than the United States, and even in the most tolerant countries both possession and puffing remain against the law and can lead to trouble if you're not careful. Always find out as much as possible before you arrive, and then talk to locals you trust to confirm these vital facts. *Is there a safe place to buy marijuana? How much should I plan to spend? Where's the best spot around to fire up a doobie?*

Next time you're abroad, leave the tourist traps behind and tap into the underground pot scene instead. Visit with local marijuana activists, stop by a headshop, or simply ask around and find the part of town that's known for its fresh greens. You'll soon discover that despite profound cultural, religious, ethnic, and economic differences, potheads all over the world stick together, not to mention roll together. So start saving your money, and in the meantime let's decide where to go, and, more important, how to score some good weed once we get there.

AMSTERDAM, THE NETHERLANDS

Only one nation on Earth treats pot smokers like respectable citizens, and fortunately for us, its crowning jewel is a charming, beautiful city with all the history, culture, art, and architecture you'd expect from a European capital. Most everyone in Amsterdam speaks English, but you should still learn at least two Dutch words before arriving: *gedogen* and *gezellig*—loosely translated as "tolerance" and "coziness," respectively.

Tolerance defines the Dutch approach to the law, which means the unique freedom they grant marijuana smokers has a lot more to do with freedom than marijuana. And *coziness* defines the Dutch way of life, as reflected in their homes, bars, restaurants, and, naturally, coffeeshops. So not only can you relax in Amsterdam because, for once, smoking herb isn't a criminal offense, but you can also relax because you're in a city that's seen it all, from Vincent Van Gogh to the *High Times* Cannabis Cup, and knows how to take it all in stride.

The Netherlands' historic tolerance of marijuana and hash dates back to the first cannabis coffeeshop in 1972, and today hundreds of such shops openly operate in the country, with the largest concentration in Amsterdam. Officially, "soft drug" sales are "tolerated," not permitted, and the government keeps coffeeshop owners on a tight leash, but any adult can legally possess personal amounts of weed without worry, and can buy and smoke up to five grams per day inside a designated coffeeshop.

Amsterdam also boasts world-class museums, food, parks, nightlife, and the most picturesque canals this side of Venice, so hit as many coffeeshops as you can while you're in town, but also be sure to come up for a breath of fresh air every so often, and see some of the city.

Amsterdam at night sparkles with stony possibility.

BARCELONA, SPAIN

Barcelonans have been inhaling hashish since the Moors invaded in the 8th century, but have only recently begun to become self-sufficient weed growers. Now they've got the best of both worlds: Cheap, potent hash remains readily available, with little hassle, plus the region's ideal climate also supports Spanish gardens full of sky-scraping, resin-soaked *sativas* that you can find on the cheap and discreetly smoke around town without too much worry. So while the rains in Spain were once known exclusively for watering the country's famous vineyards, they now fall on towering, flowering pot plants as well, thanks to a reefer renaissance sparked by a combination of increasingly friendly marijuana laws, loose enforcement, and a growing marketplace for *yerba buena*.

Best of all, Spain's second largest city knows how to party, whether you're snacking on gourmet munchies called *tapas* in the historic downtown district, scoring herb along the lively Ramblas, or taking a stoner *siesta* on the topless beaches where

Euro-lovely revelers soak up the sun all day and dance to DJ music late into the night, often under a thick cloud of smoke. Each spring, Barcelona hosts the annual Spannabis Hemp and Alternative Technologies Fair, which attracts the cream of the cannabis crowd from Europe and beyond for a combination trade show and judging competition that, like Spain's reefer scene, grows larger, and greener, every year.

Before Richard Nixon arrived, cannabis and hashish were completely legal in Nepal, home to Kathmandu's legendary Freak Street.

KATHMANDU, NEPAL

Back in the day, cannabis and hashish were completely legal in Nepal. In fact, most of the Nepalese worship Lord Shiva, a ganja-loving God of the Hindu faith. So no wonder hippies started showing up in droves in the 1960s, making the capital, Kathmandu, their first or last stop on the famed "hippie highway" that started in Europe and wound through Greece, Turkey, Iran, Afghanistan, Pakistan, and India.

Once you finally arrived on Kathmandu's famous New Road (also known as "Freak Street"), local dealers would offer you Nepalese temple balls, among the finest hashish in the universe, at incredibly low prices and with no hassle. Named for their ritualistic use within Nepal's Buddhist temples, these incredibly high-grade globes of hashish truly allowed contemplation of the infinite, much as Siddhartha (a.k.a. Buddha) survived on an all-cannabis diet before his enlightenment.

Unfortunately, everything on Freak Street changed in 1973, when Richard Nixon and agents from his newly formed DEA arrived and reportedly paid King Birendra $50–70 million to outlaw cannabis in Nepal. An ensuing shift from hashish to heroin production, coupled with ongoing internal power struggles, has taken its toll on Nepal in the thirty-five years since Birendra made his deal with the devil. Today, Maoist rebels control the marijuana-growing regions of Nepal, and use their pot profits to wrest power away from King Gyanendra, who took the throne in 2001 after the mysterious killing of the previous king and thirteen other members of the royal family.

Needless to say, Nepal isn't the pot paradise it once was, and it may never be again, but it still might be the most herb-loving place on Earth. So if you've got a taste for far-flung adventure, and want to see Freak Street firsthand, check the latest travel reports from the United Nations and make sure things are cool in Nepal before you go, or better yet, build a time machine and set it for 1970.

You haven't really experienced the mystic wonders of India until you've smoked out a wandering saddhu.

VARANASI, INDIA

According to legend, Varanasi was founded by the ganja-loving deity Lord Shiva, making it one of the seven holy cities for Hindus around the world. Also ranked among the oldest continually inhabited cities on the planet, this center of music, art, architecture, and spirituality lies on the banks of the famed Ganges River and attracts few tourists, but plenty of *saddhus*—wandering holy men who roam the Earth with nothing but a begging bowl and a *chillum*, seeking just enough food to eat and hash to smoke to satisfy the moment. Renouncing the first three Hindu goals—*karma* (enjoyment), *artha* (practical objectives), and *dharma* (duty)— the *saddhu* dedicates his (and occasionally her) life

solely to liberation from this world and contemplation of the higher plane of God. Often, this involves the sacramental use of cannabis.

Dreadlocked and penniless, *saddhus* wander across India's pilgrim routes as respected members of society, supported by donations from those they meet along the way. So, if you've been mooching weed off a friend for years, and you worry about having bad cannabis *karma*, it might be wise to make a pilgrimage to Varanasi and smoke out a *saddhu*.

Whoever made this offering to the Buddha likely gained a bit of instant karma.

KOH PHANGAN, THAILAND

Welcome to Thailand's party island, a paradise of pristine beaches, cheap lodging, and over-the-top nightlife that attracts old-school hippies, new-age spiritualists, shoestring backpackers, and hardcore hedonists. Once a well-kept secret among adventurous travelers, Koh Phangan's awe-inspiring full-moon parties sprouted up around 1987, and quickly spread the island's renown far and wide. What started out as a small, spontaneous affair soon attracted thousands during the "high season" for an all-night dance party on the beach that's truly out of this world, blending techno-rave culture, traditional Buddhist ceremony, and a healthy tolerance for cannabis.

Still, much has changed since hippies and Vietnam vets first discovered the cheap pleasures and amazing ecology of Thailand in the '60s. The world-renowned Thai stick has gone the way of tie-dye, while increasing tourism focused on sex and drugs has created a seedy industry to serve both those needs. By the late '90s, when Alex Garland set a scene in his novel *The Beach* (see page 85) on Koh Phangan, the island served as a metaphor for overdevelopment and its discontents. And most recently, conservative elements in Thailand's government have launched a bloody War on Drugs that targets dealers for execution in the streets.

Still, if you use common sense and keep a low profile, you should find plenty to enjoy in Thailand. The days of smoking spliffs in the open and finding weed cookies on the menu may have come and

An elegantly set table at Nimbin's annual Mardi Grass Fiesta and Drug Law Reform Rally.

gone, but it's not too late to score a little local grass, find a beautiful deserted beach, and *thai* one on.

NIMBIN, AUSTRALIA

This tiny dairy town was nearly deserted in 1973, when a group of radical visionaries from the Australian Student's Union arrived with plans for the first annual Aquarius Festival. After the freak fest ended, a lot of the freaks stayed on and took root, transforming Nimbin into a left-wing hippie bastion, a backpacker's destination, and something of an autonomous zone when it comes to marijuana. Although the herb remains illegal as in the rest of Australia, local officials tend to turn a blind eye to small amounts of dealing and smoking in the street.

Arrive on the first weekend in May for the "Let It Grow!" Mardi Grass Fiesta and Drug Law Reform Rally, a gathering that draws ten thousand Aussies and others to a multiday public burndown featuring political rallies, street protests, outdoor concerts, a grower's cup to judge the best local crop, and the infamous HEMP Olympics, which combines joint rolling, bong throwing, and feats of strength such as running relay races while lugging giant bags of fertilizer.

CARACAS, VENEZUELA

In 2005, Venezuelan president Hugo Chavez kicked the U.S. Drug Enforcement Administration out of his country, telling reporters that the DEA was "using the fight against drug trafficking as a mask to support drug trafficking and to carry out intelligence in Venezuela against the government." Check your highstory books, and you'll see

Australian stoners search desperately for the biggest ashtray on Earth.

he's got a point. American involvement in the Latin American drug trade dates back to the interventionist policies of the 1970s, when the United States consistently backed pro-American strongmen as a solution to populist left-wing revolutions, often despite their chosen strongman's clear ties to the lucrative cocaine trade. From the Iran-Contra scandal to Manuel Noriega to Colombia's ongoing coke-fueled civil war, Central and South America have suffered gravely from America's hypocritical War on Drugs.

So, now that the DEA's gone, Caracas must be stoner paradise, right? Well, don't start smoking in the streets, but Chavez *has* decriminalized marijuana in the country, which means Venezuela's capital now allows possession of up to twenty grams of marijuana. Nestled into a mountain valley just miles from the Caribbean sea, Caracas is also a beautiful and historic city, not to mention the center of a growing revolution in Latin American politics, where increasingly progressive governments have started to openly challenge America's War on Drugs.

MONTEZUMA, COSTA RICA

Heads in the know lovingly refer to this paradise tucked away on the bottom of Costa Rica's rugged Nicoya Peninsula as Monte*fuma*, a clever play on the Spanish word *fumar*, which means "to smoke." The best part of the local weed scene involves putting down on a carrot-sized spliff from the comfort of a hammock strung between two palm trees

overlooking an idyllic white sand beach, or better yet taking some herb with you on a ten-minute hike through the rainforest to check out the series of massive waterfalls flowing down the hillsides surrounding this small, hippie-infested town. Each waterfall culminates in a pool of cool, clean water that's just waiting to refresh you, whether you wade in carefully or dive off the surrounding cliffs.

On the other hand, the worst part of the local weed scene is the weed itself, which makes one wonder about the Spanish word for *schwag* . . . but something's far better than nothing. So how do you score in a foreign country where you don't speak the language? Start by learning a few words, one of which, *sinsemilla* (without seeds), you probably already know. Next, find one of several guys on Main Street selling wooden pipes and discreetly inform him: *Necessito verde para fumar* ("I need green to smoke"). When he quotes you a price, ask him, *"Sinsemillas?"* He will invariably say yes, even though it does have seeds, but at least he'll know that you know a thing or two about herb.

Ask to see it before you hand over the money, and feel free to negotiate, but remember: you're on vacation, so don't expect to get the local deal—at least not until you go back the next day for more.

NEGRIL, JAMAICA

If you want to see the real Jamaica, you'll have to stray from this vacation hotspot, but you can certainly get *irie* at a happening reggae night, not to mention find plenty of ganja, and plenty of ganja

NEW YORK CITY

High Times rates the best of New York City's COD (Cannabis on Demand) services

You can get anything you want in Manhattan, as long as you've got the money to pay for it. And you can get it all delivered, including some of the finest cannabis in the world. Just call the hotline when you get home from work, answer the phone when they call back, and you should be hearing the buzzer ring by the time you finish cooking dinner. Dank at your doorstep in less than an hour, that's the industry standard. Time is money, after all, and with so much competition around, the services can't afford to be late. Folks in this town hate it if you're late.

The delivery man (or woman) will generally arrive at your apartment by bicycle, after being dispatched via cell phone to your address. There will be plenty of strains to choose from, and more weight available than you'll want to buy, at least at the jacked-up prices they're charging.

When the deal goes down, it's a friendly transaction, but businesslike. You can smell, but you can't haggle. If you're polite, you'll offer a glass of water. It's not much different than ordering pizza, except more expensive and involving a lot more "oregano."

So what, exactly, do you get for your money? Good question. Fortunately, there was only one way to find out: good old investigative journalism. No more sitting here in our ivory tower, cut off from the marijuana masses—no, sir. It was high time for the *High Times* editors to hit the streets. On those streets we found people, and some of those people helped us order up delivery from the cream of New York's cannabis crop. We rated five services in each of four categories: speed of delivery, variety of strains available, price/weight ratio, and quality of product. The names of some services have been changed to protect the guilty, but we totally changed them to something similar, in case you were wondering.

The world famous New York "highline."

NEW YORK DELIVERY FAQ

Why is New York so lucky? **Because the** city is dense (in population). With so many cannabis customers per square mile, delivery in Manhattan makes sense. Gotham is also home to the kind of "high rollers" who have money to burn on high-priced, high-end hydro, marked up nicely for delivery.

When did delivery start? **Our best research** indicates the late '80s to early '90s, with the arrival of the legendary Pope of Dope (1-800-WANT-POT), although it may go back further. The industry was helped significantly by the advent of the fax machine and Mayor Rudolph Giuliani, who clamped down on NYC's traditional storefront "spots."

How do you order for the first time? **Before** placing an order, you must be referred by an existing customer.

NEW YORK STATE OF KIND

SERVICE	*Regal*	*Philly*	*Sensible*	*Karma Delivery*	*Mom & Pop's Brooklyn*
DELIVERY TIME	70 minutes	62 minutes	92 minutes	64 minutes	55 minutes
VARIETIES AVAILABLE	Great White Shark, White Widow, Hash Plant	Black Widow, Church, Trinity, Sour Diesel, Buddah's Sister	Purple Haze, Super Haze, Strawberry Haze	Strawberry Cough, Cherry AK	Haze, Mid-grade Hydro, and a ½ oz of schwag
PRICE/ WEIGHT RATIO	1.7 grams for $50	1.8 grams for $50	1.6 grams for $50	1.8 grams for $50	1.7 grams for $50
OVERALL QUALITY	"Dank basement funk," "chemy," "brisk high"	"Enlightening," "piney," "lots of crystals"	"Wasabi high," "burned well," "resinous"	"Sweet smell," "life-affirming"	"Spicy and smooth," "strong, narcotic high"
RATING	1	2	3	4	5

Top: *A bud of Lamb's Bread, Bob Marley's favorite Jamaican ganja strain.* Above: *Chef Ra,* High Times' *legendary ganja gourmet, smiles in Jamaica. Ra wrote his "psychedelic kitchen" column from 1988 until his untimely death in 2006.*

dealers, right on Negril's Seven Miles beach, or working in your hotel, or bringing you Red Stripes at the bar, or cooking your jerk chicken on a portable grill, or braiding your hair, or driving your taxi in from the airport.

Basically, you'll have no problem finding grass, hash, and ganja cake, but remember, you're the naive tourist, and they're the locals, so expect a few people to try to rip you off with the bad deals they foist off on inexperienced smokers who don't know any better. As for the herb: The powerful native *sativas* that Bob Marley blazed as a young man have all been replaced with crossbred hybrids that yield fatter buds in a shorter time span, but there's still fantastic outdoor ganja to be found in Jamaica, particularly if you take the time to shop around. Some of the strongest strains may appear brown or even schwaggy, but the discerning nose will discover their powerfully dank scent. If you see lots of red hairs, that's the good stuff. And be forewarned—Negril space cakes are notoriously potent, so eat at your own risk and don't go swimming for at least three hours after ingesting. Also, weed may be everywhere, but it's illegal, and corrupt cops sometimes target potheads for bribes, so be discreet when buying and smoking, and don't deal with anyone who makes you feel uncomfortable. Save your ganja dollars for the nice guys.

If Negril sounds a little too "spring break" for your tastes, arrange a guided tour of Ganja Mountain. You'll discover better deals, and friendlier people, the farther you get from the rest of the tourists.

ANN ARBOR HASH BASH

In 1969, an attractive undercover policewoman in Ann Arbor, Michigan, arrested John Sinclair for possession after he passed her two joints' worth of marijuana, and a court sentenced him to ten years in prison. Fortunately, Sinclair, a young radical activist connected to the White Panther Party and the music group MC5, had some friends in *high* places, including Beatle legend John Lennon, who wrote a song for Sinclair and performed it at a freedom rally to protest his sentence. Three days after the concert, Sinclair was freed from prison, and the Michigan Supreme Court later overturned his conviction.

Today you can find John Sinclair presiding as the occasional master of ceremonies at the Ann Arbor Hash Bash. Now well into its third decade on the University of Michigan campus, the Bash has been held every year on May 1 to celebrate Sinclair's freedom. Best of all, activists from the movement to free Sinclair not only started the party, but they also spread the love to the whole city by passing an ordinance in 1972 making marijuana possession only a civil infraction punishable by a $5 fine (since raised to $25).

Now that's a cause for celebration.

BOSTON FREEDOM RALLY

Masscann.org

For nearly two decades, Massachusetts's freedom-loving pot patriots have hosted a modern-day

The Ann Arbor Hash Bash is held every year on the campus of the University of Michigan.

"Boston Tea Party" every year on the third Saturday in September. The largest marijuana event on the East Coast, better known as the Boston Freedom Rally, evokes the city's revolutionary past for a free outdoor festival for Beantown's weed enthusiasts that includes a full day of speakers, booths, music, munchies, and mingling.

THE EMERALD TRIANGLE

When you think potatoes, you think Idaho. When you think corn, you think Iowa. And when you think marijuana, you should think California, most notably the legendary Emerald Triangle formed by Mendocino, Humboldt, and Trinity Counties. Cut off from the rest of Northern California by forests of giant redwood trees, the Emerald Triangle enjoys an ideal climate for cannabis cultivation, and has represented the epicenter of American herb growing and breeding since the earliest days of homegrown. Today, with California leading the way toward both medical marijuana and outright legalization, the hills are more alive than ever with the smell of ganja.

Arrive in the autumn and look for work during harvest season, when each of the millions of lovely pot plants grown in Northern Cali have to be cut down and meticulously trimmed by hand. Experienced clippers can earn good money for their services, tax free, plus a place to crash, all you can smoke, and plenty of munchies—all in one of the most beautiful stretches of unspoiled land left in America. Now, where did I leave those scissors?

ABOVE: *The Northern California coastline sure looks lovely from high up in the Humboldt hills.* OPPOSITE: *Quick scissors find steady work in Northern California come harvest season. Even if you don't make the cut and land a gig, it's certainly a lovely time of year to take a vacation.*

SEATTLE HEMPFEST *Hempfest.org*

Only five hundred heads attended the first Seattle Hempfest in 1991, held in undersized Volunteer Park, but even then, organizers knew they were "sowing seeds" that would one day flower into a

ABOVE: *A majorette weilds a major joint on the poster for Seattle Hempfest 2002, designed by Jaime Sheehan and Art Chantry.* OPPOSITE: *Maple Leaf marijuana.*

much larger event. Today, Hempfest draws crowds of 250,000 to the beautiful downtown Seattle waterfront for two days of celebration, protest, lobbying, music, food, art, and plenty of good vibes.

Tommy Chong, Snoop Dogg, Woody Harrelson, Jack Herer, Rick Steves, Mark Stepnoski, and a veritable who's who of activists and organizers in the marijuana movement have all made the trip to

Seattle for America's largest reefer rally. If you've got friends in the marijuana movement, you'll find them here. If not, it's a great place to make some.

VANSTERDAM

The massive plane, boat, truck, and helicopter loads of "BC bud" that arrive in America every year take their name from Canada's westernmost province, and all that exporting makes marijuana a big business in British Columbia, which, not coincidentally, includes Vancouver, the greenest big city in North America, and an excellent budget option for stoners who can't quite afford to make the pilgrimage to Amsterdam just yet. Hit "Vansterdam" instead, and you can spend your "high holiday" making world-class snowboarding runs in the nearby mountains, trekking through the amazing Pacific Northwest rainforest, swimming on a nude beach next to the University of BC campus, or relaxing downtown, enjoying some of the cheapest and best sushi in the world.

Of course, if you're looking to roll up something a little stronger than raw fish while in Vancouver, try Hastings Street, where a small cluster of cannabis coffeeshops awaits. You can't score inside, but you'll find a mix of tourists and locals lighting up and scarfing down on munchies in a chilled-out atmosphere, and while there's nowhere to legally buy weed in Vancouver, police definitely have more important priorities than people selling or even smoking pot in the street. Anyway, Canadians are amazingly accommodating, and unlike

in America, there's no reason to be paranoid, so rather than deal with the dealers, why not wait until you meet a friendly local who can hook you up properly with some killer buds?

You won't be dry for long.

HIGH TIMES DOOBIE AND STONY AWARDS
Location changes annually; www.hightimes.com

Oscars and Grammys may look impressive on the mantle, but *High Times'* homegrown awards statues double as functional bongs. No wonder some of the biggest names in music, movies, and television have shown up to get their hands on our highest honors: the annual Doobie Awards for music and Stony Awards for entertainment. Presenters and performers over the years have included Snoop Dogg, Sean Paul, Dave Chappelle, Redman, Doug Benson, and many more.

ABOVE: *Cannabis Cup judges must sample dozens of strains before choosing the world's best pot. Nice work if you can get it!* OPPOSITE: *According to legend, whoever catches the Cannabis Cup bouquet gets really, really stoned.*

HIGH TIMES CANNABIS CUP
Amsterdam, The Netherlands; www.cannabiscup.com

Inspired by the legendary California harvest festivals of the 1970s, the annual *High Times* Cannabis Cup is a heated battle to determine the best herb and hash in the world. It started in 1987 with only three judges and four contestants, but after twenty years of rapid growth, the Cup has evolved to include dozens of coffeeshops and seed companies, more than fifty varieties of cannabis and hashish, a giant paraphernalia trade show, expert grow seminars, seed breeding competitions, Counterculture Hall of Fame inductions, Freedom Fighter of the Year awards, and high-profile entertainment for the thousands of pot pilgrims who arrive from all over the world to have their votes counted.

Celebrity judges and musical guests have included Rita Marley, Jack Herer, Sebastian Bach, Alex Grey, Patti Smith, Fishbone, the Kottonmouth Kings, Galactic, Jefferson Starship, 311, and Steel Pulse.

WHO'S
THE MAN?

Okay, let's be honest: This is the section of the book that we all wish wasn't necessary. In a rational, sane, just, or even explicable world, weed would be legal for adults, and that would be the end of it. Clearly, however, when it comes to cannabis, the world is irrational, insane, unjust, and inexplicable, and so we need to talk about the marijuana laws, and most important, how to change them.

In the United States, roughly 1.5 million people are arrested each year for drug violations—40 percent of them just for marijuana possession. The money spent and lives wasted on this prohibition against a beneficial plant may seem crazy, but the War on Marijuana affects countless otherwise law-abiding citizens every year, in America and all across the globe. Some pay small fines, some get a free ride in a police car, some have their property confiscated, and some end up in prison. As a result, instead of utilizing an amazing cash crop for our fledgling family farmers, we squander precious resources on incarceration and enforcement in a never-ending battle to prop up the losing side of a pointless campaign against a harmless pleasure. There's a lot more to the story, of course, but that's the gist.

Che Guevara (yes, the guy from the T-shirts) once said: "The first responsibility of any revolutionary is not to get caught." All reefer revolutionaries need to take this motto to heart. If you really want to end pot prohibition, it starts with not becoming a victim of pot prohibition yourself. Learn the facts, let common sense guide you, and never think it will never happen to you, because it always could. And even if it doesn't, we stoners still share the responsibility for our own liberation. As long as any one of us is punished for smoking herb, then none of us is truly free.

The good news is that you don't have to change the world all by yourself. Activists of all kinds (yes, pun intended) would love to meet you and explain the many ways to join them in finally winning our freedom. We're turning the tide and gaining more of our rights every year, so there's never been a

better time to get involved than right now. Read this chapter carefully and then get in touch with a marijuana law reform organization that's right for you. The pot smoker you save could be yourself.

In the meantime, let's answer a few of the most frequently asked legal questions from *High Times* readers.

WHY IS POT ILLEGAL?

It's a long story (see Chapter 1, "Highstory"), but it's mostly due to a combination of racism, fear-mongering, profiteering, social control, and the maintenance of the status quo at any cost. The early propaganda campaigns that led to the first American prohibitions against marijuana painted horrifying pictures of dark-skinned, reefer-smoking homicidal maniacs chasing after all the white women in town. In the conformist '50s, one puff of pot could instantly transform any upstanding young person into a filthy beatnik, and possibly a communist. By the time the '60s rolled around, marijuana became associated with the antiwar movement, the environmental movement, the gay rights movement, the women's liberation movement, and other social justice causes—again, a threat to the powers that be. Then pot made you lazy. Then it made you do hard drugs. Then it made you a terrorist. Since the charges against cannabis keep changing and contradicting each other, we can only assume that a powerful medicinal plant that can't be patented, makes you want to share, and leads a lot of us to question authority . . . well, somehow this miraculous healing herb tends to make those in authority more than a little nervous. Not to mention paranoid.

"They're going to talk to you and talk to you about individual freedom," Jack Nicholson's character noted in *Easy Rider*, shortly after getting stoned for the first time. "But if they see a free individual, it's gonna scare them."

Dennis Hopper: "Well, it don't make them running scared."

Jack Nicholson: "No, it makes them dangerous."

Basically, marijuana's not antiestablishment because it's illegal, it's illegal because it's anti-establishment. Pot makes you ask questions and imagine another way the world might be made better and more fair. And that has always made the people in power afraid of us.

WHO WANTS POT TO REMAIN ILLEGAL?

So now you understand how these horrible laws got on the books in the first place, but after seventy years of failed policy, wasted money, and ruined lives, how can we go on and on with this bullshit? A huge majority of Americans support medical marijuana, and a clear majority think that recreational reefer should be decriminalized too, so why haven't the laws caught up with the will of the people?

"Follow the money" far enough, and you'll see that some nasty people are making some serious money off of keeping pot illegal.

🌿 LAW ENFORCEMENT

The pigs have lined up at the trough at every level, from the DEA on down to your friendly local cops, and they all want their share of the $7.7 billion spent annually on marijuana enforcement. Because of financial incentives from the federal government, busting stoners, dealers, growers, and smugglers leads to asset seizures, new equipment, and bigger budgets for all the boys on the force. And so,

Federal agents with the Campaign Against Marijuana Planting (CAMP) demonstrate the exact wrong way to harvest a crop.

Getting caught with this plant can turn your life upside down

Getting caught with a marijuana plant in your home can land you in jail for several years with a felony conviction.

Marijuana smokers are no longer arrested in eight states. The U.S. Congress and many other states are considering similar reforms.

But growing any amount of marijuana remains a serious crime in most states and under federal law. It means that 15 million regular smokers are forced to support an illicit market.

This doesn't make sense to us.

Smokers should be permitted to grow their own marijuana. Cultivation for personal use should be decriminalized. A proposal to do just that is pending in California and will soon be introduced in Oregon.

Write your state and federal elected representatives. Tell them you support decriminalizing private marijuana cultivation for personal use.

Help make the new marijuana laws come out right side up.

JOIN NORML.

Money is needed to finish the job once and for all.

sprout

while most citizens stay up nights worrying about violent crime, global warming, and hard drugs, the police devote a disproportionate amount of their limited time toward arresting nearly a million marijuana smokers per year, mainly because it's easy and lucrative.

✿ PRISON INDUSTRIAL COMPLEX

In America, the erstwhile "land of the free," private companies make a tidy profit off of incarcerating more citizens per capita than any other nation on Earth. The War on Drugs makes sure these facilities stay full and that more get built every year, providing marijuana offenders with free housing, free food, and free health care from the government, all at taxpayer expense. Any attempt to curtail this "revenue stream" meets with intense opposition from Wackenhut Corporation, Corrections Corporation of America, and other major players in the profitable world of private prisons, not to mention the corrupt politicians who take these companies' huge campaign contributions and then do their bidding in Washington, D.C.

✿ THE MILITARY

The U.S. military has become increasingly involved in the international narcotics trade since Richard Nixon first declared a War on Drugs in 1968, including extensive eradication efforts in foreign countries and intensive efforts to stop marijuana from arriving in America from Mexico, Canada, and elsewhere. Instead of stemming the tide of supply, however, these misguided efforts at stopping overseas production and sealing the border

ABOVE: *A U.S. soldier in Afghanistan told* High Times *he first smelled this massive pot plantation from a few miles away.* OPPOSITE: *A NORML ad from the 1970s.*

have only led self-reliant stateside stoners to start growing their own, making homegrown, all-American marijuana the envy of the world.

✿ PHARMACEUTICAL COMPANIES

What if a plant with amazing healing properties grew for free from the earth with no patent, and no profit for the pharmaceutical companies? Would they see it as a blessing for society or as unwelcome competition? Don't kid yourself—the pharmaceutical companies make multibillion-dollar profits every year and don't have any desire to see marijuana muscling in on their turf, despite the fact that it's been proven an effective treatment for patients with cancer, AIDS, multiple sclerosis, glaucoma, arthritis, and other serious illnesses.

Always pack carefully when traveling with marijuana.

Check out the major donors to Partnership for a Drug-Free America and other pot prohibition organizations and you'll find a who's who of legal drug pushers like Johnson & Johnson, Procter & Gamble, and Bristol-Meyers Squibb.

CAN I REALLY GET IN TROUBLE FOR SMOKING POT?

The answer depends entirely on where you're getting high. In Singapore, potheads have faced the death penalty for a few grams of grass, while in Alaska you can pretty much puff in peace as long as you possess only personal amounts. Most places in America, a first-time arrest for small amounts

of marijuana won't bring more than a fine, but it's always important to know the deal where you are before lighting up, even if you're only passing through. Check out NORML's state-by-state guide to marijuana laws on its Web site, www.norml.org.

HOW CAN POT BE BANNED WHEN TOBACCO AND BOOZE ARE PERFECTLY LEGAL?

You can ask the question a million different ways and never get a straight answer. You'll get answers aplenty, of course, but they'll just be complete and utter bullshit. Here's a rundown of the three most popular artful dodges used by the drug warriors, and their myths debunked.

GATEWAY THEORY: Marijuana leads to hard drugs.

MYTH DEBUNKED: Statistics prove that the real gateway is alcohol. Also, it's marijuana *prohibition* that exposes pot smokers to the wider black market and its other illicit offerings.

SOCIETAL THEORY: Alcohol and tobacco are accepted parts of our society, making them fundamentally different from marijuana.

MYTH DEBUNKED: Precedent is no excuse for bad policy. Slavery and child labor were once accepted parts of our society, along with opium-laced baby medicines.

ENOUGH PROBLEMS ALREADY THEORY:
Alcohol and tobacco are bad enough, so why add to our troubles?

MYTH DEBUNKED: Marijuana is by far the least harmful of the three. Also, millions of Americans already use cannabis regularly. And most marijuana-related problems stem from the *prohibition* against it, not its use.

IS MEDICAL MARIJUANA LEGAL?

As of 2008, twelve states have approved laws allowing their citizens access to marijuana for medicinal purposes. Most of this legislation originated as voter initiatives placed on the ballot by medical marijuana activists and passed by the vast majority of citizens aware of the overwhelming scientific and anecdotal evidence proving that smoking cannabis helps patients with a wide range of serious illnesses. Still, the federal government recognizes none of these state laws and ignores all evidence in support of medical marijuana, pointing to a 2005 Supreme Court ruling (see "Supreme Disappointment" page 159) that established federal prohibition as superseding any state's protections, effectively making medical marijuana illegal even in cases where it's a matter of life and death.

Despite this seriously flawed ruling from the so-called High Court, the movement to make medical marijuana legally available to anyone with a doctor's recommendation makes strides each year, especially in California. Since 1996, Proposition 215 has required the state to issue medical marijuana cards to approved patients, allowed medical growers to cultivate a regulated amount of plants on behalf of these patients, and prompted independent cannabis dispensaries to distribute all this kind medicine to those in need. No longer forced to seek relief in the black market, pot patients can now choose from hundreds of openly operating dispensaries ready to serve their needs with high-quality cannabis, plus marijuana-infused food and tinctures for those who have trouble inhaling. Many dispensaries offer not only medicine,

For many patients suffering from cancer, AIDS wasting syndrome, multiple sclerosis, and other chronic illnesses, medical marijuana means the difference between life and death.

but also patient–based support groups and holistic health care.

Technically, all of this activity remains illegal, but aside from the relatively few instances when the *federales* decide to get involved, the system works and works well.

HOW CAN I HELP?

You can get involved by joining up with medical marijuana activists wherever you live, whether it's helping to start a ballot initiative in your state, or lobbying Congress to end the federal prohibition against medical marijuana once and for all. For as long as these laws have been enforced, dedicated activists have been working hard to change them, either by educating their fellow citizens, lobbying their elected officials, or engaging in civil dis-obedience and public protest. Marijuana smokers represent a massive voting block of millions of con-cerned Americans from all walks of life and every demographic—rich and poor, young and old, black, white, Hispanic, and every shade in between. We've been persecuted for more than seventy years, but the times they are truly a–changin', and if we all learn to roll together for reform, nothing can stop us from achieving our freedom.

This one time, at band camp, we got really stoned....

Each of the organizations that makes up the "grassroots" marijuana movement has a different approach to making our dreams a reality, but all of them can and will make you part of the "green" team. And remember, getting involved not only feels great and creates positive change, it's also an excellent way to make kind new friends who share a common interest.

Pot protestors take to the streets to free the weed.

NATIONAL ORGANIZATION FOR THE REFORM OF MARIJUANA LAWS (NORML)

Founded: 1971
www.norml.org

Not only is NORML misspelled, it's highly inaccurate, as the oldest and largest marijuana reform organization in America actually represents an extraordinary group of activists willing to donate their time, money, and reputations to the cause of cannabis freedom. With a large base of small donors, NORML's heavily involved in all aspects of reform, including medical, legislative, and educational campaigns, while always retaining its focus on issues of concern to America's recreational pot smokers. Join them as a paying member, or simply volunteer your time, and you'll help work toward NORML's stated goal of "moving public opinion sufficiently to achieve the repeal of cannabis prohibition so that the responsible use of this drug by adults is no longer subject to penalty."

In addition to the national office in Washington, D.C., NORML supports more than one hundred state and local chapters, including many on college campuses. NORML advisory board members have included Hunter S. Thompson, Robert Altman, and Rick Steves.

🌿 STUDENTS FOR SENSIBLE DRUG POLICY (SSDP)

Founded: 1998
www.ssdp.org

A small group of young, dedicated activists started up SSDP following the enactment of a provision to the Higher Education Act that banned federal financial aid to anyone with a drug conviction—even for simple possession of a single joint—but imposed no such sanctions against serial killers, arsonists, or crooked politicians. Check out page 162 for the *High Times* interview with Kris Krane, SSDP's executive director, and get the full story on how the nation's fastest-growing student organization has already partially repealed the Aid Elimination Penalty, and how they plan to take it all the way down.

Speak loudly and carry a big joint. Marijuana advocates fight the power.

SAFER ALTERNATIVE FOR ENJOYABLE RECREATION (SAFER)

Founded: 2005
www.saferchoice.org

SAFER's very name begs the question: Which is safer, alcohol or marijuana? A cursory glance at the number of deaths caused per year by each substance (alcohol: around 100,000, marijuana: 0) should answer the question once and for all, and yet we all know where the law comes down on this subject. Starting out on college campuses, and working up to a ballot initiative for the entire state of Colorado, SAFER has been bypassing the politicians and putting the question directly to the voters. Check out page 164 for the *High Times* interview with SAFER co-founder Mason Tvert, and get the full story on how his organization managed to legalize the herb in the city of Denver.

MARIJUANA POLICY PROJECT (MPP)

Founded: 1995
www.mpp.org

Beware of any organization whose stated goal is "minimizing the harm associated with marijuana." Flush with money from major donor Peter Lewis, head of Progressive Insurance, MPP plays the role of insider lobbyist, cultivating relationships in Washington with an establishment-friendly image that may make less buttoned-up stoners feel a little underdressed for the party. MPP also uses its largesse to fund state ballot initiatives and scholarly research, not to mention throwing the occasional gala bash featuring celebrity supporters like television host Montel Williams, who smokes medical marijuana to treat his multiple sclerosis.

MULTIDISCIPLINARY ASSOCIATION FOR PSYCHEDELIC STUDIES (MAPS)

Founded: 1986
www.maps.org

Wouldn't it be cool if they did experiments with psychedelic drugs to see if they could possibly help people, and heal people, rather than trying to keep it all under wraps? Some of the oldest and most advanced cultures on Earth incorporated ritualistic use of psychedelic drugs into their societies as a kind of spiritual medicine, and MAPS founder Rick Doblin thinks we should find out why. MAPS has already gotten FDA approval to study MDMA-assisted psychotherapy in the treatment of post-traumatic stress disorder, undertaken the first study analyzing the effectiveness of marijuana vaporizing, won a lawsuit against the DEA for its refusal to license a MAPS–funded medical marijuana production facility, and struggled for six years to start the first human study in over fifteen years on the medical use of cannabis (which received $1 million in federal government funding). In late 2007, MAPS obtained final approval for the world's first LSD psychotherapy study in more than 35 years, to treat people with anxiety from life-threatening illnesses.

Talk to these guys if you want to turn on the world from the inside out.

LAW ENFORCEMENT AGAINST PROHIBITION (LEAP)

Founded: 2002
www.leap.cc

Modeled after Vietnam Veterans Against the War, which used the credibility of combat veterans to denounce an unwinnable and disastrous conflict, LEAP membership is open only to cops, DEA agents, prosecutors, and other accredited law enforcement officers. Most members wait until they retire from the force before taking the leap into the opposition, as dissension in the ranks is not tolerated in the War on Drugs. So if you're a cop, and you know firsthand the horrible hypocrisies of drug prohibition, please join up with LEAP and help everyone come to their senses. You owe it to every citizen you were forced to fuck with because of a system that's out of control. And if you're not a cop, thank your lucky stars that there are men and women out there brave enough to risk their reputations by telling the awful truth about the War on Drugs.

AMERICANS FOR SAFE ACCESS (ASA)

Founded: 2002
www.safeaccessnow.org

An Oakland–based organization at the heart of the fight for medical marijuana in California and beyond, ASA now claims thirty thousand members, comprising chapters in over forty states. Working in partnership with local, state, and federal officials, ASA has helped the modern medical marijuana movement make amazing strides, including a successful lawsuit against the California Highway Patrol to end the confiscation of medical cannabis and make "CHiPs" officers otherwise comply with the mandates of Proposition 215. ASA also works with politicians and local patients and providers to help implement sensible and secure protections for medical marijuana dispensaries. And they're often the first ones out in the street protesting whenever the federal government decides to raid a medical grower, a successful media counteroffensive that has made the DEA reluctant to endure the bad press that each bust generates.

Join ASA, and you join the largest organization working solely on medical cannabis.

DRUG POLICY ALLIANCE (DPA)

Founded: 2000
www.drugpolicy.org

A large umbrella organization overseeing a multitude of specific projects, the DPA believes that the War on Drugs causes more harm than good and envisions a future where citizens are not punished for what they put into their bodies, but only for harm done to others. As the name implies, they're mostly interested in drug policy, specifically the way the laws against drugs are written and the real-world effects of those laws once they're unleashed on the public.

DPA formed from the merger of a think tank and a grant-making organization, so expect serious people, serious money, and an extremely serious focus on reversing the largest public policy disaster of our time.

BLACK TUNA: 27 YEARS IN THE CAN

Almost three decades after making the cover of *High Times*, Robert Platshorn remained America's

Robert Platshorn with his wife and son, just prior to serving 27 years in federal prison. Learn more at www.blacktunadiaries.com.

longest-serving marijuana prisoner. Better known as inmate #00603–004 at the Maxwell Air Force Base Federal Prison Camp in Alabama, Platshorn may also be remembered by a few longtime *High Times* readers as leader of the Black Tuna Gang, convicted in 1980 of heading the "biggest and slickest" drug ring in U.S. history. The case against the Tunas represented the first joint effort between the DEA and FBI to investigate profits from the marijuana trade, a campaign that showcased many tactics the drug warriors have honed and expanded over the ensuing years: sleazy paid informants, so-called expert witnesses, selective prosecution, inflated statistics (see: amount of drugs, street values, size of profit . . .), overt propaganda, naked self-promotion, and most of all, a policy of heartless ass-covering that would make War on Drugs founder Richard Nixon proud.

Meanwhile, Platshorn—a first-time, non-violent offender who hadn't taken his son fishing since he was 4 years old—spent 27 years in the can. Matthew Platshorn, now in his 30s, works as a special education teacher in Nevada. He was waiting by the phone when his father finally got released, and some other poor soul earned the dubious distinction of being the longest-serving prisoner of war in the War on Marijuana—a transition that took place on April Fools' Day, 2008.

So how did this family man ever get started in the black market for greens?

"I think it was the atmosphere of the '70s. It seemed it was almost legal. The first time someone came to me and said, 'I have 500 pounds; do you know anybody who wants it?'—that was a very attractive proposition," Platshorn told *High Times* in 2005. "At that time, the average first offender would get three to five years, and usually that would be a suspended sentence. I never thought anyone was serious about putting people away for a long time for marijuana. I honestly thought pot was going to be legalized. That we were only a few years away."

We were not. The modern War on Marijuana was just getting started and, in fact, still had something to prove. Operation Banco, that first-ever DEA/FBI joint effort, had burned through a lot of time and taxpayer money delving into the dirty dealings going down in Miami in the late '70s, only to see the big fish somehow slip through their nets. Along the way, these strange bureaucratic bedfellows jilted some fellow feds, namely the IRS and Customs, who were reportedly undertaking investigations of their own—into the failures of Operation Banco.

The rest is obvious to anyone who knows how the Drug War is fought and lost in America: Somebody had to go down, *hard.*

Nobody doubts that the Tunas were moving serious weight. Platshorn fondly recalls flying down to Santa Marta, Colombia, to score planeloads of the good stuff from well-connected local Raul Davila-Jimeno, a.k.a. the elusive Black Tuna, who, for the record, was nowhere to be found when the heat came down on the Tuna Gang that took his name. In the beginning, the pot was great, the profits were great, and so were the people. And so Platshorn figured: Why not?

"It was fun when it was a business that had acceptance, when it looked like pot was going to

Robert Platshorn, a.k.a. "The Black Tuna," poses with his vegetable art.

be legalized, and when we dealt with hippie types—nice people who were fun to be around, and did not have guns. All of that collapsed when they made it very clear that pot was going to be a serious crime."

Platshorn was indicted on May 1, 1979, along with his wife and eleven other members of the extended Tuna family. His home was raided at gunpoint and his children were placed in protective custody. U.S. Attorney General Griffin Bell announced the indictments at a national press conference, turning on the heat for a media campaign aimed at searing the Tunas in the fire of public opinion. Prosecutors also trotted out the Racketeering Influenced Corrupt Organizations (RICO) Act and charges of a "continuing criminal enterprise"—two heavy-duty measures intended to take down organized crime, which were turned against the decidedly disorganized crime of the Tunas (see *High Times*, September 1981: "The Gang That Couldn't Deal Straight").

Throughout the trial, the government issued press releases designed to create the palpable perception of major wrongdoing—accusing the Tunas of hoarding hundreds of millions of dollars, commanding a private army, and plotting to kill the judge. Naturally, the newspapers all went along for the ride.

"We made a modest amount of money," Platshorn admits, "but not even 1 percent of what was alleged. [The government claimed] anywhere from one million to three million pounds were brought in, but at trial the reality was less than one hundred thousand pounds. In total, we made three flights, plus a boat trip. And all of a sudden we're the biggest thing that ever hit marijuana."

When the sentence came down—sixty-four years—you can bet those boys on the joint task force were laughing all the way to the Banco. The DEA/FBI juggernaut credited their original failed operation with taking down the nation's largest drug ring, and promptly returned triumphantly to Washington, D.C., with their hands out for more Drug War money. Meanwhile, both Platshorn and his wife went to prison, and although her sentence was only a few years, Platshorn says she's never really recovered. Then his daughter died at age 12 of an epileptic coma. Then both his parents passed on. And now, most recently, his younger sister has died as well. All the while, the government supplied Platshorn with free housing, health care, and three hot meals a day.

So sure, he's learned his lesson. But what if way back when he'd received a big fine and a slap on the wrist? "If we had gotten a reasonable sentence, I can't imagine that we'd have gotten back into the business. We had already stopped before we were indicted, and didn't bring in so much as a seed for two years," Platshorn says, claiming he'd already seen the writing on the wall—the Feds were dead serious about pot, bigger fish were moving in, and the glory days of multiton shipments were over. "I read all the articles in *High Times* about homegrown, and all the ads for grow lights, and that definitely seemed to be where it was going. There was no reason to smuggle that kind of bulk into the United States anymore."

SUPREME DISAPPOINTMENT

After a tough loss in the High Court, the battle for medical marijuana moves on to Congress

Attention all interstate herb traffickers: The U.S. Supreme Court has got your back. How else to explain the High Court's 2005 ruling in *Raich v. Ashcroft*, a 6–3 decision confirming the federal government's right to regulate (i.e., outlaw) medical marijuana—even in the states where voters have specifically enacted laws to make it legal?

So what's the Court's rationale for this massive expansion of federal powers? *Interstate commerce.* Basically, the justices in the majority argued that medical marijuana represents a threat to the nationwide market in illicit marijuana sales (by reducing demand), and therefore the Feds have grounds to intervene because the "commerce clause" of the Constitution explicitly grants them the power to regulate commerce between the states.

"It seems rather ironic to appeal to the fact that homegrown marijuana would reduce the interstate commerce that you don't want to occur in order to regulate it," Justice Antonin Scalia noted during oral arguments, though he eventually voted with the majority anyway. "I mean, you know, doesn't that strike you as being strange?"

Strange indeed, but as they say in legal circles—not without precedent. The rationale for this leap of logic arrives via *Wickard v. Filburn*, a Depression-era court case that found a farmer arguing unsuccessfully that the wheat he grew and consumed on his own land ("head wheat") was not subject to the taxes and regulations placed on commodities sold in the marketplace. In the case of

Angel Raich continues to use medical marijuana to treat a range of life–threatening illnesses, despite her defeat in the U.S. Supreme Court.

medical marijuana patient Angel Raich—a chronically ill woman who suffers from fibromyalgia, endometriosis, scoliosis, asthma, and an inoperable brain tumor—the cannabis she smoked on doctor's orders was grown on her own property, completely in compliance with California state law. At no time were these plants bought, sold, traded, or transported across state lines, but somehow six of the highest authorities in our judicial system still managed to convince themselves that this activity comprised interstate commerce, and thus provided cover for the DEA to enter California and enforce the Controlled Substance Act (CSA), which acknowledges no medical use for marijuana whatsoever, classifying it as a Schedule I substance alongside heroin, crystal meth, and LSD.

"This marks the end of medical marijuana as a political issue," Drug Czar John Walters gloated shortly after the decision, relishing the fact that the Supreme Court's overruling of the Ninth Circuit Court of Appeals had now given him and his Drug War cronies free rein to once again raid the homes of patients and the farms of medical suppliers. But raids and arrests alone will hardly end medical marijuana as a political, medical, legal, or social issue.

In fact, despite ruling against Raich, Justice John Paul Stevens offered a specific remedy for patients, physicians, activists, and others frustrated by efforts to win over the judiciary: take your complaints to Congress. "We do note the presence of another avenue of relief. As the Solicitor General confirmed during oral argument, the statute [CSA] authorizes procedures for the reclassification of Schedule I drugs," Stevens wrote in the majority opinion. "We acknowledge that evidence proffered by respondents in this case regarding the effective medical uses for marijuana, if found credible after trial, would cast serious doubt on the accuracy of the findings that require marijuana to be listed in Schedule I. . . . But perhaps even more important than these legal avenues is the democratic process, in which the voices of voters allied with these respondents may one day be heard in the halls of Congress."

You heard the judge: First step, contact your local representatives and lend your voice in support of legislation like H.R. 2087, the "States' Rights to Medical Marijuana Act," which would use the power of Congress to protect statewide laws establishing medical marijuana programs by changing the scheduling status of cannabis. The act continues to gain support and additional co-sponsors as it winds its way through the legislative process, and may soon gain enough momentum for an up-or-down vote in Congress. If it passes, medical marijuana supporters will have a victory larger than the Supreme Court defeat, and if it fails, they'll try again and again until it passes.

So take heart, because despite this temporary setback, most Americans still agree that medical marijuana should be legal. They also recognize that the government's prohibitions are based on callous lies, and once the cowardly politicians in Washington realize this they will quickly begin to act in their constituents' best interests, instead of at the behest of compassionless bureaucrats like John Walters.

"Before going to the Supreme Court, I felt if I lost this case, I would surely have to leave the USA to stay alive," Angel Raich told *High Times* shortly after her day in court. "But I realized that I am not done fighting here. I plan to take this battle to Congress next. It is time that the federal government grows up. Medical-cannabis patients are not going away, and the federal government better get used to it!"

JUST SPRAY NO *Is Sativex the future of medical marijuana, or a mist opportunity?*

For the first time in history, a cannabis-derived pharmaceutical has been officially accepted for medical use, and wouldn't you know it—those freewheeling Canadians were the first ones in line. Sativex, an oral spray produced by United Kingdom–based GW Pharmaceuticals, is now available by prescription to Canadian patients suffering from multiple sclerosis, for combating episodes of "neuropathic pain" associated with that degenerative condition.

The manufacturers of Sativex—which is extracted from naturally cultivated *Cannabis sativa L.* plants—are currently running clinical trials to prove their elixir's effectiveness in alleviating a wide variety of additional ailments traditionally treated with medical marijuana, and have even founded the highly official-sounding Cannabinoid Research Institute to lead their research and development efforts.

The principal active components in Sativex, delta-9-tetrahydrocannabinol (THC) and cannabidiol (CBD), have been known and synthesized since 1964, but until now the only pharmaceutical available has been Marinol—a completely artificial version of THC created in a laboratory, which does not contain cannabidiol or any other therapeutic components of cannabis and is ineffective for many patients helped by medical marijuana. Sativex, on the other hand, derives from a "whole plant extract," prepared at a secret cultivation facility in Britain, and contains all active ingredients in a measured dose from a quantifiable plant grown under strict scientific supervision—the kind of setup prohibition makes nearly impossible, at least on a large scale.

And so Sativex sounds great so far, and will undoubtedly prove beneficial for patients given access, but before we all run off and light up our victory joints, let's ask a few necessary questions:

1. Why are the two cannabis extracts listed as active ingredients in Sativex (both naturally occurring compounds within the plant) suddenly registered trademarks of GW Pharmaceuticals, and what does that mean for anyone else interested in innovating in the field of cannabis medicine—particularly when GW boasts to potential investors about their "aggressive approach to securing intellectual property rights" in areas including "plant variety," "methods of extraction," "drug delivery device," and "methods of use"?

Dr. Geoffrey W. Guy, founder of G.W. Pharmaceuticals, "experiments with marijuana" in the United Kingdom–based company's secret research facility.

2. Will medical marijuana patients be forced to pay GW the kind of huge markups pharmaceutical companies traditionally demand to offset the cost of manufacturing, packaging, distribution, research and development, public relations, marketing, corporate profits, etc., just to end up with a "pharmaceutical" that grows like a weed for free? Here's what GW founder Dr. Geoffrey Guy has to say on the subject: "My definition of a pharmaceutical is a worthwhile medicine that will make money."

Now ask yourself: How would Pfizer react if they found out you were growing fields of Viagra in your backyard?

Bonus Question (Worth Double): Does the arrival of Sativex herald the end of marijuana prohibition as an absolute and the beginning of a reality-based debate followed by a slippery slide into outright legalization, or does it signal quite the opposite—the beginning of the "pharmaceuticalization of marijuana," with the immensely powerful multinational pharmaceutical industry moving in to control the world's cannabis, armed not with criminal sanctions but corporate lawyers?

CITIZEN KRANE *The* High Times *interview with Kris Krane, executive director of Students for Sensible Drug Policy*

Kris Krane began his career in drug law reform as a student at American University in 1997, a year after California citizens passed Proposition 215 in support of state-sanctioned medical marijuana, and a year before Congress passed the Higher Education Act (HEA) "Aid Elimination Penalty," which denies federal financial aid to any student convicted of a drug crime (though murderers, arsonists, and drunk drivers can all still apply). Over the course of the next decade, Krane worked his way up from student intern to associate director at the National Organization for the Reform of Marijuana Laws (NORML), and now on to his new gig as executive director of Students for Sensible Drug Policy (SSDP), weathering the ups and downs of the movement along the way, while earning a reputation as an organizer with the ability to inspire young activists to fight back against the Drug War. In his new role, he'll oversee both the national SSDP headquarters in Washington, D.C., and almost fifty campus chapters nationwide.

Working with the American Civil Liberties Union, SSDP has recently launched a lawsuit challenging the constitutionality of the HEA penalty in federal court. "If we're successful," Krane told *High Times*, "no student will ever have to worry again about losing their financial aid due to a drug law conviction."

How did you first get involved in drug law reform?
I attended a NORML meeting and then joined a protest with my NORML chapter when Barry McCaffery, who was the Drug Czar at the time, visited our campus, but I didn't really delve in until my senior year when I did my honors thesis on drug policy, asking why we continue to escalate a policy that has clearly failed. When I researched my thesis, I started to understand just how pervasive and detrimental the Drug War is in all aspects

of society, particularly to young people, poor people, and minorities. That's when I got heavily involved with the SSDP chapter on my campus, then started interning for NORML, and I've been following that path ever since.

Have you ever been personally affected by the Drug War?

My father used medical marijuana when I was a kid, as he was essentially dying of a rare form of emphysema. He used to tell me at the time that he smoked joints because it helped him breathe by opening up his lung passages. He passed away when I was only 8 years old, so at the time I had no idea what that meant, but later, I put two and two together and realized that a joint was marijuana and this was the stuff that helped my father live more comfortably in the last year of his life. That was a real wake-up call, and definitely the most personal experience that got me involved in this issue.

Kris Krane, executive director of Students for Sensible Drug Policy (SSDP).

The Drug War is based on belief and ideology, rather than facts. Do you really hope to change your opponents' minds, or just build up an effective opposition?

There are some drug warriors out there who are true believers, but the vast majority of them are just career politicians doing what they believe is the politically popular thing to do, so if we can change the minds of the people, they will listen, because otherwise they will be voted out of office. It's our job to reach a critical mass in public opinion so that elected officials start to realize that it's no longer political suicide for them to come out

in favor of reform, and we've already started to see that with some of these issues. When elected officials and career bureaucrats realize that the majority favors drug law reform, they will change their positions. These are politicians, after all.

How effective has the HEA been as a recruiting tool for SSDP?

SSDP actually started in 1998, the same year the Higher Education Act Amendment was signed into law by President Clinton. This was around the advent of the Internet, and a lot of student activists started discussing the new provisions online, got really motivated, and formed a new organization dedicated specifically to students. We've seen a lot of people become involved specifically because of this issue, and once they start trying to change this HEA law, they get hooked and become activists for life.

What makes this new generation of activists unique?
To be honest, I see a lot of professionalism among the young activists today. I've been almost surprised to find that students don't join these organizations because they want to find a good party—although activism can and should be fun—but because they have a desire to change the law. One of the best things I see is that there are a lot more women involved. If you look at the old guard of the drug law reform movement, it's very male dominated, but when you look at the leadership of the campus chapters of SSDP, I'd say it's about a 50/50 split.

SAFETY FIRST *SAFER's Mason Tvert likes marijuana a lot more than booze*

Mason Tvert and Steve Fox co-founded Safer Alternative for Enjoyable Recreation (SAFER) in January 2005, following two alcohol-related deaths on Colorado's college campuses, arguing that undergraduates (most of whom are too young to drink legally) should not face more severe penalties on campus for toking than they do for getting drunk. Their reasoning struck a chord, and both targeted campuses quickly passed "alcohol equivalence" initiatives supported by SAFER.

The activists then ran a successful legalization initiative in the city of Denver (yes, *mile high* indeed), and then, in November 2006, expanded the battlefield again, this time organizing a ballot initiative for all of Colorado that would have legalized up to an ounce of herb for adults. Although that effort fell short, with 41 percent of the vote, SAFER took on the Drug Czar, state cops, and everyone else in support of the status quo while sparking a real debate on marijuana legalization.

Tvert, 25, sees the statewide setback as a necessary step in a long campaign that's rapidly gaining momentum.

What about SAFER's message attracted you?
My senior year in high school, I had a very serious drinking incident where I almost died. I drank way too much, went to the hospital—the whole ordeal—and I didn't get cited for anything, I didn't get arrested, I didn't have anyone get involved, except my parents. All my friends just thought it was cool that I'd gotten so drunk. Then I went to college, and became one of many people investigated for marijuana by a multi-jurisdictional grand jury, which involved campus, local, state, and federal police, including the DEA.

So on the one hand, I almost drank myself to death, and no one cared, and on the other, I might or might not smoke a little pot, and every level of government gets involved. I thought that was totally absurd, and that we need to start educating young people immediately about these two drugs because they should know that marijuana is less harmful than alcohol.

How has that comparison been received by the public?

Our message has resonated across Colorado since we started with the local initiatives. We've picked up not only statewide interest, but also national interest. When the initiative passed in Denver, we even picked up attention internationally, which means people hear our message: Marijuana is safer than alcohol.

And how has the establishment reacted?

Our opponents are forced to keep changing the dynamic of the debate. They had to account for our arguments, and in some cases admitted that marijuana is less harmful. So this approach points out their hypocrisy while educating people about marijuana use. We boil it down to: *Why is marijuana so much worse than alcohol that no one can have it?*

We want people to start asking questions, and many have no frame of reference. They don't use marijuana or they don't know anything about it, but they drink, or they have friends who drink. We need a way to relate to people and get them thinking in a new way, because that's what it's going to take for real reform. We're not out to change the laws so much as change people's minds and let them change the laws. And so we say: *Hey, marijuana's like drinking, but without the violence and hangovers.*

What did you learn from the statewide initiative process?

I learned a lot. This was our first time dealing with well-funded, serious, organized opposition, including the Drug Czar and other federal entities. It was interesting to see just how much the supporters of these marijuana laws will do to

Mason Tvert, co–founder of Safer Alternatives for Enjoyable Recreation (SAFER).

keep them the same. In my opinion, our opponents were slimy and unethical, using taxpayer dollars to oppose our initiative. But that didn't surprise me so much as the lack of attention to these activities. The press doesn't question enough whether these tactics are legal. And this is important, because if you take all these federal and state law enforcement groups out of the debate, our opposition is basically nothing. This is really a case of the people vs. their own government.

RELEASE THE HOUNDS! *Who let the dogs out? The Supreme Court, that's who.*

A canine can be trained to search for the scent of illegal drugs, or it can be trained to detect the presence of dangerous explosives, but it cannot be trained to do both—at least not at the same time. In other words, given a world in which a limited number of dogs will be trained, every dog trained for antinarcotics work equals one less antiterror dog available to sniff out explosives down at the airport. Economists call this an opportunity cost. More accurately, in this case, an opportunity lost.

After all, do you lie awake at night afraid that someone might be smuggling high-grade marijuana across the Canadian border? Of course not: You just hope they don't jack up the price too high once they reach the land of the free. Now picture that same van loaded with weapons, packed up and ready to go. Now the threat is real. Now you want that dog working the border, ready to lay down his

life to thwart a terrorist attack. Too bad he's been trained to sniff out the half-ounce of BC bud in your glove compartment instead of the dirty bomb in the trunk of the car behind you.

Speaking of glove compartments, that's a pretty bad place to store your stash during vehicular travel. May we recommend the trunk, instead? Also, you might want to consider investing in a vacuum sealer (also great for leftovers) and sealing up your shit tight before hitting the road—particularly now that the Supreme Court has sicced the dogs on your ass. That's right, thanks to a 2005 ruling from the so-called High Court, the cops can now have a canine check out your car anytime, anyplace—even if they have no particular reason to suspect illegal activity.

Welcome to the American Police Dog State.

The Supreme Court decision stems from the case of Roy Caballes, who was pulled over on Interstate 80 by an Illinois state trooper for traveling six miles an hour above the posted speed limit. The officer on the scene became suspicious upon encountering a well-dressed man in an empty, out-of-state car that smelled strongly of air freshener, and asked for permission to search the vehicle. Caballes, mindful of the 282 pounds of marijuana stored in the trunk, declined the request and was on the verge of getting off with a warning when another officer arrived with a police dog in tow. The dog "alerted" in the vicinity of the trunk, and a search ensued, followed by an arrest and a conviction.

The case was subsequently thrown out by the Illinois Supreme Court, which found that the use

Not all drug sniffing dogs work for the government.

of the dog constituted an unwarranted and therefore unlawful search of the defendant's private property. And so Caballes would have gotten away with it, too—if it hadn't been for those meddlesome U.S. Supreme Court justices.

In a later decision, the so-called High Court ruled 6-2 that a drug dog sniffing outside your trunk doesn't actually constitute a search, since the only thing the dog might possibly detect is the presence of illegal drugs, which you don't have a right to keep private in the first place. And since it's not really a search, it's perfectly legal. For Caballes, this bit of reasoning led directly to a twelve-year prison sentence. For the rest of us, only time will tell.

Ever wonder what became of Herbie the Love Bug?

DRIVE CAREFULLY *Seven rules of the road for motorists carrying precious cargo*

🌿 **POWER VACUUM** Dude, you need to get a vacuum sealer—especially if you're carrying around more herb than you'd care to answer for in a court of law. These miracle devices store your greens airtight, keeping them fresh, and better still, lock in all aromas, making them the ideal gadget for heads on the go. They're also popular among the foodies of the world and will therefore raise no eyebrows at the point of purchase— unless, of course, you ask which brand works best for weed.

🌿 **KEEP THE FUNK IN THE TRUNK**
Just because that ounce of OG Kush has been vacuum-sealed and therefore rendered odorless, that's no reason to drive with it sitting in your lap. A locked trunk can only be searched by police with probable cause, while other areas of your car—anywhere a gun might be accessible, for instance—are fair game. So buy yourself a small safe disguised as a water bottle and hide it in a cooler in the trunk.

🌿 **NO SMOKING** First of all, no matter what you tell yourself, your driving does not improve when you're stoned—it's just that the music sounds a lot better. Also, getting high in the car increases your chances of getting pulled over, and the odor and appearance of pot smoking greatly increases your chances of a search.

🌿 **NO SPEEDING** Duh.

🌿 **GO INCOGNITO** The Grateful Dead have millions of fans and have played music live before more people than anyone else in history. Their musical legacy will survive without your bumper sticker, and you will stand a far better chance of surviving a routine traffic stop without that Steal Your Face above your license plate.

🌿 **KNOW THE LAWS** If you're traveling across state lines, take the time to review the various laws to which you will be accountable, so you can make an informed choice about what to bring with you in the car. Also, consider driving around Oklahoma.

🌿 **DO NOT CONSENT** If you are asked to consent to a search, politely say no. The police seek your permission only when they do not have legal grounds to search without it. Stay calm and explain that you are heading to an important appointment and that you need to get moving as quickly as possible. Do not be intimidated or coerced into surrendering your rights. If you're not sure whether you can leave, simply ask, "Am I free to go?"

GOVERNMENT-GROWN GRASS

A timeline of federally supplied medical marijuana

 1968
The U.S. National Institute of Mental Health (NIMH) establishes the Drug Supply Program to provide clinical investigators with cannabis, THC, and other controlled substances for medical research, contracting with the University of Mississippi to grow marijuana for the program. To this day, UMiss remains the only legal supplier of cannabis for clinical research.

🌿 **1974**
Congress establishes the U.S. National Institute on Drug Abuse (NIDA), which takes over as administrator of the existing cannabis contract and sole supplier of legal cannabis in the United States.

🌿 **1978**
NIDA supplies cannabis cigarettes to glaucoma patient Robert Randall under the newly established Compassionate Investigational New Drug (IND) program. Thirteen patients eventually receive NIDA pot under the program and dozens more receive preliminary approval before its abrupt closure in 1992. Of the original thirteen IND patients, seven are alive and continue to receive medical cannabis monthly from NIDA.

🌿 **1979**
NIDA begins providing medical cannabis to patients approved under New Mexico's Lynn Pierson Therapeutic Research Program—the first state-authorized medical marijuana research trial. Six states—California, Georgia, Michigan, New York, Tennessee, and Vermont—establish similar programs. The studies conclude that cannabis therapy is equal to or better than the oral administration of synthetic THC.

1985

The U.S. Food and Drug Administration approves the oral THC pill Marinol as a legal prescription medication. Shortly thereafter, NIDA ceases to provide marijuana for state-sponsored clinical research.

1998

Requests by the state health departments of Massachusetts and Washington to NIDA seeking marijuana for state-authorized research are unsuccessful.

2004

NIDA Director Nora Volkow affirms it is "not NIDA's mission to study the medical uses of marijuana."

Since 1968, the federal government has used a research facility at the University of Mississippi to grow legal medical marijuana, supplying clinical trials and a handful of approved patients. Unfortunately, those with firsthand knowledge tell High Times that the package that arrives in the mail each month contains prerolled joints of low potency, poorly grown shake—nothing like the beautiful buds pictured above. We keep offering to send a few cultivation consultants down to Mississippi, but the Feds never get back to us . . .

THE *HIGH TIMES* GUIDE TO HIGHER EDUCATION

Take the official tour of any college or university, and you'll soon find yourself strolling through the quad, visiting a dorm room, marveling at the size of the library, stopping in for a "not-so-bad" lunch at the cafeteria, and even meeting a hand-selected student made available to answer your questions about life on campus. Feel free to inquire about the guy–girl ratio, fraternity life, or the percentage of undergrads who eventually go on to attend graduate school. Just don't ask the one question that's probably at the foremost of your mind: Is this a good school for stoners (like me)?

America's institutions of higher education would soon come to a grinding halt without marijuana smokers, including students, professors, deans, administrators, maintenance workers, and the coach of the women's field hockey team, yet these same colleges and universities are understandably none-too-eager to publicize their population's participation in this important (albeit illicit) aspect of academic life. That's where your high-minded friends at High Times *come in handy.*

Each autumn, we rank the top schools in the country (and Canada) from the cannabis community's point of view. Most recently, with the help of Students for Sensible Drug Policy (SSDP) executive director Kris Krane, we put the emphasis on activism, particularly when it comes to ending America's long and disastrous War on Marijuana.

As Krane and everyone else intimately involved in the struggle to declare peace and end the Drug War knows, we need a new generation of dedicated, educated activists ready and eager for a "head-on" collision with our nation's misguided marijuana policy and the corrupt system that supports it. If you feel like you're up to the challenge of freeing the weed, you'll certainly be sure to find some kindred spirits at one of our Top Ten Cannabis Colleges.

HONOR ROLL

 ## UNIVERSITY OF MICHIGAN
Ann Arbor, Michigan
www.umich.edu

During the presidential election primary season, University of Michigan SSDP brought two presidential candidates, Dennis Kucinich and Mike Gravel, to speak on campus. Kucnich's speech was his largest campaign stop in the state. The chapter also attended an Office of National Drug Control Policy drug testing summit, where they convinced school administrators and teachers not to implement random drug testing programs in their schools. In 2007, the chapter became the only first-year group ever awarded SSDP's Outstanding Chapter Award.

 ## FRANKLIN PIERCE UNIVERSITY
Rindge, New Hampshire
www.franklinpierce.edu

When faced with an overzealous local police department that locked suspected marijuana smokers out of their dorm rooms without a warrant, Franklin Pierce University's SSDP chapter held a protest on campus that attracted not just fellow students, but also members of the school administration. Shortly afterward, the university canceled the practice of warrantless police searches of the dorms. The chapter also hosted the 2008 SSDP Northeast Regional Conference in April, and two chapter members currently serve on SSDP's national board of directors.

 ## BROWN UNIVERSITY
Providence, Rhode Island
www.brown.edu

Brown University, which features the longest running continually active SSDP chapter in the country, has done more to change local drug policies than many professional organizations. Brown and University of Rhode Island SSDP members have joined forces to form the Rhode Island Patient Advocacy Coalition (RIPAC), which in 2006 successfully lobbied the Rhode Island Legislature to pass a state-wide medical marijuana law. Currently, they're pushing a bill that would permit government licensed medical cannabis dispensaries. In 2007, Brown hosted the SSDP Northeast Regional Conference, which featured former United States Senator Lincoln Chaffee.

 ## UNIVERSITY OF CENTRAL FLORIDA
Orlando, Florida
www.ucf.edu

One of the largest and longest running NORML chapters in the country, not to mention one of the best funded organizations on campus, UCF NORML has gained a reputation for bringing high-quality speakers to campus, including NORML director Allen St. Pierre, NORML founder Keith Stroup, *High Times* associate publisher Rick Cusick, SSDP executive director Kris Krane, and federal medical marijuana patient Irv Rosenfeld. In early 2008, UCF NORML ran a successful SAFER initiative in which students voted to lower campus marijuana penalties to equal those for underage drinking.

Students, stoners, faculty and townies all come together to celebrate 4/20 at Farrand Field, on the campus of the University of Colorado in Boulder.

SSDP Board of Directors, and is a starting outfielder for the SSDP/NORML One Hitters in the Congressional Softball League.

 ## ROOSEVELT UNIVERSITY

Chicago, Illinois
www.roosevelt.edu

A largely commuter-based school located in downtown Chicago, Roosevelt University has hosted symposiums featuring some of the world's most renowned experts on medical marijuana. The SSDP chapter has also played key roles in producing well-publicized research reports, including one on racial disparities in the Illinois prison population, co-authored by national SSDP Board Members Jennifer Janichek, Kathleen Kane-Willis, and Allison Grimmer that garnered front-page coverage in the *Chicago Tribune*.

 ## UNIVERSITY OF CONNECTICUT

Storrs, Connecticut
www.uconn.edu

The University of Connecticut SSDP chapter was among the first groups in the country to convince their school administration to adopt a Good Samaritan Policy, protecting a student from punishment for a drug or alcohol offense if they call security to assist a dangerously intoxicated friend or colleague. SSDP chapter leader Dan Cornelius currently serves on the national SSDP board of directors, has lobbied the Connecticut state legislature in support of medical marijuana legislation, and won SSDP's Outstanding Activist award in 2007.

 ## UNIVERSITY OF MARYLAND

College Park, Maryland
www.umd.edu

The University of Maryland represents a model of collaboration between SSDP and NORML chapters. The two clubs routinely hold joint meetings and coordinate events together. After running a successful SAFER initiative in 2006, UMD SSDP and NORML engaged in a two year lobbying campaign to lower the school's marijuana penalties, finally resulting in the administration ceasing the practice of evicting first-time marijuana offenders from campus housing. UMD SSDP chapter president Stacia Cosner has testified multiple times before the Maryland State Legislature, serves as vice-chair of the national

MISSOURI SOUTHERN STATE UNIVERSITY

Joplin, Missouri
www.mssu.edu

Over the past year, Missouri Southern State University's SSDP/NORML chapter has brought an effective voice for drug policy reform to conservative southern Missouri. The chapter teamed up with Joplin NORML to place an initiative on the November 2008 ballot that would make marijuana possession the city's lowest law enforcement priority. On campus, the chapter recently won a hard fought endorsement from the University Senate.

UNIVERSITY OF MEMPHIS

Memphis, Tennessee
www.memphis.edu

As NORML's only official affiliate in the state of Tennessee, the University of Memphis NORML chapter has been petitioning the Tennessee State Legislature to establish a panel to study medical marijuana, convinced that any such commission will convince the legislature to legalize medical marijuana in the state. The group has been hosting film screenings, DJ nights, and other fundraisers to drum up support for the initiative on campus.

AMERICAN UNIVERSITY

Washington, D.C.
www.american.edu

SSDP executive director Kris Krane got his start in activism at American University, home to one of the founding SSDP chapters in 1998. These days, American's chapter organizes outings to lobby members of Congress to repeal the law that denies financial aid to students with drug convictions. American University will be hosting SSDP's 10th annual national conference in November 2008.

ABOVE: *At High Times' top 10 colleges, even the pigs know how to party!* PAGES 176–177: High Times *readers of the world, unite!*

WHERE DOES MARIJUANA COME FROM?

Here's the good news: They call it *weed* for a reason. Cannabis has one of the strongest life forces of any plant on Earth, and thrives in almost every imaginable climate, from the highest reaches of the Kush mountains in Afghanistan to the arid near-deserts of the Middle East to the dank depths of the tropical rainforests of South America, and, of course, in basements, closets, attics, greenhouses, and anywhere else clever indoor cultivators can find to hide their love away.

In nature, marijuana is an annual plant, with seeds that germinate in the spring, develop rapidly during the summer, bud and flower in the autumn, and produce new seeds that fall to the ground and begin the process all over again. This cycle has been repeating for millennia, so if you're thinking about planting some herb of your own, you should take great comfort in the fact that Mother Nature has been successfully propagating *Cannabis sativa* since a time long before anyone came along to name it. (And yes, by any other name, it would still smell as sweet . . .)

Simply provide your plants with proper light, air, water, and nutrients, and they will flourish, producing the kind of fat, sticky, resin-coated buds you've grown accustomed to drooling over in the pages of *High Times*. Give them *all* the love they deserve, and you can yield enough to put yourself (or your kids) through college, but as soon as you neglect any one of these elements, your ganja will suffer, and so will your harvest. Also, because of society's misguided prohibitions, you'll have to keep your garden a secret, which can involve anything from scouting the ideal planting location in the middle of a remote patch of sticker bushes to adding air filters to your basement grow room to keep the smell of fresh grass from wafting up to the neighbors.

In the end, growing pot isn't right for everybody, or most people, or even most stoners, but for the chosen few it can be a wonderful way to commune with the herb and make some serious tax-free money at the same time. Know the risks and the rewards in advance, research thoroughly where, when, and how you would grow, and then make an informed decision. If you choose to take the plunge, start small and do it right, so you will have something to show for all your effort and risk.

With a lot of planning, and a little luck, you'll soon discover that there's absolutely no better feeling in the world than smoking some killer buds that you grew yourself.

ABOVE: *A fully state-sanctioned medical marijuana farm in Northern California.* OPPOSITE: *When people say they look down on pot growers, this usually isn't what they mean.*

INDOORS VS. OUTDOORS

Cultivating a successful garden—*especially* a marijuana garden—requires a lot of planning, and the first big decision remains the most important: *Where should I plant?* Keep in mind your crop's basic needs—light, air, soil, water, and nutrients—and figure out the easiest, safest, and most efficient means to supply them. Start by deciding how much you want to yield, and how much time, money, and energy you're willing to invest to reach that goal.

The biggest advantage of growing outdoors is that sunlight's free, which means no money up front for high-intensity lights and no monthly electric bill. Air circulation should also be no problem. Water and nutrients can be supplied by the rain and the soil, but Mother Nature can't be expected to baby your plants the way you would in an indoor grow room, which means outdoor marijuana is often subject to less light, fewer nutrients, and the constant risk of flood or drought. Still, cannabis is an amazingly vital species, and if your outdoor plants take root, you'll likely yield a nice harvest without much work, hassle, or worry.

So why bother with indoors? While you'll need to fork out in advance for a bunch of equipment and gauges, this total mastery of the garden will allow you to give your plants exactly what they need, exactly when they need it, while nipping any potential problems in the bud. Keep the lights on eighteen hours per day for rapid vegetative growth and then decide exactly when to switch over to the 12-and-12 light cycle that induces flowering and starts the process of forming fat buds.

TOP: *Indoor gardens allow for total control of the environment.*
ABOVE: *Greenhouses offer growers the best of both worlds.*
OPPOSITE: *Whoever said growing weed isn't hard work never had to harvest.*

Top: *Male plants develop telltale pollen sacks.*
Above: *Female pistols form on an adolescent marijuana plant.*

Whether you decide to grow indoors or outdoors (or not at all), always plan before you plant, and give your garden the loving attention it deserves. A healthy harvest will be your reward.

SEED YA LATER

Spanish for "without seeds," *sinsemilla* growing describes the process of producing the highest-grade ganja possible by planting only females and keeping them all frustrated virgins until harvest. This may sound a bit cruel, but dig it: Only female plants produce appreciable amounts of the THC-soaked resin that gives marijuana its magical powers; they produce it specifically to attract the pollen of the males; and they *keep on* producing it up until they're pollinated, at which point they switch over their energy to forming seeds to ensure another year of existence.

So when you're growing weed, it's all about the ladies. Male plants not only don't get you high, but they're not to be trusted in the garden. One male can easily ruin an entire grow room, halting the process of resin production and turning your high-grade girls into a seedy mess.

Since the '70s, clever cannabis cultivators have known that planting cuttings from an elite female plant guarantees that all herb in the garden will be lovely ladies, with gooey resin to spare. Start by germinating ten seeds and growing them until the seedlings develop sex organs (see photos at left). Get rid of the males immediately, and then eventually select the best of the females to be your "mother plant." Grow the mother plant for a few weeks, and then start taking genetically identical clones by cutting off stems from the bottom and replanting them in small containers. Once you have a large, healthy mother plant, you can keep her alive, and keep taking clones off her, for many years.

The most sophisticated grow operations have one area dedicated to raising clones and a much larger space devoted to flowering, ensuring a perpetual harvest every few weeks. No boys allowed!

GUERRILLA GARDENS

A guerrilla army attacks where it's not expected, secures victory, and then disappears without a trace—which is exactly the approach you should take to a guerrilla garden. Plant where it's not expected, on a remote patch of land far from prying eyes, secure victory in the form of a fat harvest of buds, and then disappear without anyone being the wiser.

Much like real estate, the three most important factors in a guerrilla garden are *location, location, location*. You must choose a spot with adequate sunlight, soil, air, water, and drainage; close enough to visit at least twice a month, but also remote enough that no one will stumble across it, including hunters, hikers, rival growers, or a friendly local park ranger. You won't have as much access or control as you would with a backyard or indoor garden, but there's less risk than planting on your own property, and at far less cost than growing indoors.

The Money Shot—a male pot plant pollinates an eager female.

First, scout out your patch, preferably well in advance so you can visit it several times to see if it gets consistent sunlight all season and to make sure your plants will blend in well with the surrounding vegetation until an autumn harvest. Select a strain that thrives in your outdoor climate, and start by growing a set of clones until they're about six inches tall. Next, pay your patch a visit, without any pot on your person, and make any necessary improvements, such as pulling weeds, adding fertilizers, or trimming overhead vegetation.

When you're ready to plant, moisten the clones and pack them carefully into a backpack along with a small shovel, enough soil to transplant

INDICA VS. SATIVA

Regardless of whether two different species evolved from the same genus or one species split along geographic lines, by the time humans discovered how to get high, cannabis had already separated into two easily distinguishable lines, with sativas *growing wild in almost all equatorial regions of the globe, and* indicas *thriving in Southern Asia and the Indian subcontinent. In each case, the plants were eventually discovered, recognized, cultivated, and bred for their desired characteristics—*sativas *for straight smoking, and* indicas *for making hashish and* kif. *This process went on undisturbed for thousands of years, without the two lines ever crossing paths, until a combination of far-wandering hippies, the Grateful Dead, and the U.S. War on Drugs brought them together for the first time.*

From the 1920s until Nixon declared an all-out War on Weed in the 1970s, most of what ended up filling our star-spangled bongs arrived by way of Mexico and South America, smuggled across a loosely patrolled border. Check out a copy of *High Times* from the early days, and you'll see a steady stream of imported *sativa* strains with names like Panama Red, Punta Roja, and Acapulco Gold. Our own founder, Tom Forcade, used to personally fly planeloads of Colombian into the country, then known as the strongest smoke on the market.

Once Uncle Sam started cutting those southern supply lines, however, the large demand for high-grade marijuana, combined with the vacuum in supply created by border patrols and overseas interdiction, eventually ignited the grand tradition of American ingenuity, and soon the country's entrepreneurial spirit made the emergence of a thriving homegrown crop almost inevitable. The only problem: The equatorial *sativas* everyone

knew about wouldn't grow well inside the United States, particularly the farther north you traveled. Around the same time, however, hippies who'd been following the famed hashish trail from Afghanistan to Nepal started returning home with seeds, including a new kind of cannabis plant—*indica*. Shorter, heartier, more drought resistant, and bred for thousands of years to produce the resin required to make hashish, the indica plant was an ideal match for American soil, particularly in Northern California, the epicenter of the stateside seed-breeding scene.

It wasn't long until enterprising farmers began crossing *indica* with *sativa* to produce hybrids featuring the best of both worlds—the smooth smoke, fragrant taste, and clear, soaring high of *sativas*, paired with the stout buds, hearty growth, early flowering, and heavy stone of the *indica*. The bitchinest of these crosses were wind blown across the country via the traveling Grateful Dead parking lot scene, with some of the most legendary and enduring strains in the world of cannabis making their name in this time period, including: William's Wonder, Trainwreck, and Skunk #1.

Most modern marijuana horticulturists prefer plants that tend toward the *indica* side, mostly because they grow short and fat with thick buds, producing far greater yields in far shorter time periods than *sativas*. But that doesn't make *indica* a better smoke. Ask any pot snob worth his pipe, and he or she will tell you that ounce for ounce there's no finer herb in the world than a purebred *sativa* like Burmese, Nigerian, or Colombian.

For first-time growers, however, *High Times* recommends starting off with a hearty *indica* that will give you a nice, heavy yield, along with allowing some room for error while you learn the art and craft of cannabis cultivation. Find a seed company you trust, and ask them for a good beginner's strain with some Northern Lights in it.

🌿 A TALE OF TWO SPECIES 🌿

SPECIES	*Indica* 	*Sativa* 
NATIVE REGION	Southern Asia and the Indian sub-continent (Afghanistan, Pakistan, India, Tibet, Nepal)	Equatorial climates (Mexico, Thailand, Colombia, Jamaica, Vietnam)
FLOWERING TIME	6–8 weeks	11–13 weeks
ACTIVE INGREDIENT	High levels of CBD, producing a heavy body "stone"	High levels of THC, producing a clear, soaring "high"
PHYSICAL CHARACTER-ISTICS	Thick leaves; short, stout plants; thick buds. Average height: 2–4 feet	Thin leaves; tall stretchy plants; wispy buds. Average height: 5–10 feet
FAMOUS EXAMPLES	Northern Lights, Blueberry, MK-Ultra	Panama Red, Thai Stick, Haze

each clone, and a large bottle of water. Like a guerrilla warrior, you should plan to avoid detection. Visit your patch early in the morning, and have a cover story ready in case you need one, like a dog on a leash, or a copy of Thoreau's *Walden*.

Work quickly, without rushing, and try not to leave a trail when walking to or from your patch. Maintenance depends on the climate. If you receive adequate rain, you may not need to visit your guerrilla garden again until harvest, though you may be disappointed by what you find if heavy storms, grazing deer, insects, or infectious mold have taken their toll.

When the big day finally arrives, plan your harvest as carefully as your planting, especially considering the hopefully large bag of evidence you'll be lugging home.

Organic ganja tastes great, smells sweet, and just might save the world!

DON'T PANIC, IT'S ORGANIC

Synthetic fertilizers and pesticides largely consist of petroleum, which contributes to global warming, depletes natural resources, degrades farming soil, and makes crops increasingly susceptible to insects and infections. Organic growing, on the other hand, benefits the soil and leads to hardier, healthier harvests, which explains why more and more consumers have been "going organic" when it comes to eating, opting out of a food chain that chooses the convenient and profitable over the healthful and sustainable.

Growing organic ganja may not save the world, especially if you're only cultivating a small garden, but it will certainly help. You'll also harvest buds that smell sweet and taste fantastic. Organic ganja is especially important for medical marijuana users who may react negatively to the chemical residue left behind by synthetic fertilizers or pesticides.

Ask around at your local garden store, and they'll be glad to turn you on to a whole world of organic alternatives—just don't tell them what exactly you're growing.

ANIMAL FARMERS *Five critters that contribute to cannabis cultivation*

☙ BATS

Bat guano (or bat shit) has a high phosphorus ratio that makes the stuff essential for growing great organic, resin-soaked buds. Maybe it's the steady diet of bugs, or maybe it's all that sleeping upside down in caves, but either way this poop packs a punch—and pot plants are just batty for it.

☙ LADYBUGS

Don't be deceived by cute appearances: ladybugs are carnivores, and voracious ones at that. Unleash a package of these hunters in your grow room and watch aphids and other harmful insects run for their lives.

☙ SEA BIRDS

Again, it's potent poop we're after. Whether Peruvian, Malaysian, or off the Jersey shore, all sea birds drop guano rich in the nutrients needed for vegetative and flowering stages of growth. The best way to collect it is by either putting on a clean, white shirt or eating an ice-cream cone on the beach.

☙ PREDATOR MITES

Got an infestation in your garden? Why spray your medicine with dangerous, chemical pesticides when you can let loose these mighty warriors instead? Predator mites show no mercy. They will kill the bugs *and* eat their eggs. Just make sure they don't come after you.

Ladybugs must get the "munchies," because they eat plant pests for breakfast, lunch, and dinner.

☙ FISH

Rotten fish has been used in fertilizer since civilization first made the transition from hunting and gathering to agriculture, and while liquefied fish may stink to high heaven, the nitrogen levels and trace nutrients within make this a must-have elixir for the discriminating gardener. So, does something smell fishy? *Yeah, it's called great weed.*

LIVING NIGHTMARES *Five pests that plague pot production*

🌿 SPIDER MITES

Fucking spider mites! Nature's ultimate weed mooch, eating up your plants and kicking down nothing in return but an infestation nightmare.

🌿 DEER

Yes, these are graceful, gentle creatures, but after watching an outdoor crop slowly disappear—bite by tiny bite—amid a traffic jam of deer prints, you'll be more in the mood to rent *The Deer Hunter* than *Bambi*.

🌿 MOLD

What are you, mold? A plant? An animal? Why do you even exist? What possible motivation do you have to wake up in the morning and be mold, unless it's another day of ruining a beautiful garden?

🌿 WHITEFLIES

Insects like whiteflies are an integral part of our planet's ecosystem, helping to maintain the delicate balance of life that sustains us all. Which is all well and good until these little bastards start eating your budding beauties. Then it's war.

🌿 PIGS (i.e., "THE POLICE")

Not all cops are pigs, but let's face it: this is one animal infestation you'd rather not have in your garden. Unfortunately, cop-repellent sprays have proven ineffective, and these suckers are too big to be eaten by predator mites.

Whiteflies and deer can turn your budding beauties into a green salad.

HEMP, HEMP, HOORAY!

Cannabis sativa L. subspecies *sativa* variety *sativa* sounds like some kind of futuristic space-weed, but you wouldn't want to smoke it. That's actually the specific variety of hemp grown legally in Europe, Canada, China, and elsewhere around the world for food, fuel, and fiber. Industrial hemp contains only trace amounts of THC (0.3 percent by Canadian standards), which means you'd have to ingest a ton of the stuff in one sitting to get anywhere near the effect found in today's high-grade grass.

TRANS HIGH MARKET QUOTATIONS (THMQ): THEN AND NOW

Ever since our premiere issue, High Times *has served the needs of value-conscious cannabis consumers with up-to-the-minute Trans High Market Quotations (THMQ), a reader-compiled index of current marijuana prices in America and beyond. Needless to say, inflation's a bitch.*

NOVEMBER 1974 (ISSUE #1)

Kabul, Afghanistan
Afghani Primo: $2 per ounce

Kingston, Jamaica
Lambs Bread: $60 per pound

Paris, France
Moroccan Hash: $40 per ounce

Amsterdam, The Netherlands
Congolese Black: $100 per ounce

Tel Aviv, Israel
Blond Lebanese: $5 per ounce

New York City
Vietnamese: $45 per ounce

MARCH 1979

Colombia
Santa Marta Gold: $10 per ounce

Northern California
Thai Stick: $150 per ounce

SEPTEMBER 1982

Saudi Arabia
Black Kashmir Hash: $250 per ounce

Sikeston, MO
Commercial Colombian: $525 per pound

NOVEMBER 1987

Memphis, TN
Mexican *Sinsemilla*: $100 per ounce

Austin, TX
Skunk: $35 per ¼ ounce

FEBRUARY 1990

Bloomington, IL
Indoor *Indica*: $40 per ¼ ounce

Tampa, FL
Sativa "Big Buds": $25 per ¼ ounce

APRIL 1994

Boulder, CO
Kind Buds: $80 per ¼ ounce

Westfield, MA
Northern Lights: $60 per ⅛ ounce

JULY 1997

Enid, OK
Purple Sticky Hairs: $90 per ¼ ounce

Bend, OR
Double Skunk: $275 per ounce

JUNE 2008

Tucson, AZ
White Rhino: $360 per ounce

Athens, TN
Hashberry: $400 per ounce

 ## NATIONAL GROSS MARIJUANA PRODUCTION

UNODC numbers for 2003–2004 (most recent available)

Morocco: 16,000 metric tons (42%)
North America: 14,000 metric tons (33%)
Africa: 12,000 metric tons (28%)
South Asia: 4,000 metric tons (9%)
Central Asia: 2,250 metric tons (5%)

LICENSED INDUSTRIAL HEMP
BIOMASS RESEARCH PLOT

THIS IS **NOT** MARIJUANA (0%THC)

PLEASE DO NOT DISTURB
FOR SURVEILLANCE
& OTHER INFORMATION
CALL 613-395-2690

Keep off the grass . . . uh, hemp. . . .

Evidence of humans utilizing hemp dates back to the Stone(d) Age, when hemp fiber strengthened pottery in China. For the next twelve thousand years, this most versatile plant served humanity in the manufacture of textiles, shoes, ropes, and paper. Thomas Jefferson wrote his original draft of the Declaration of Independence on hemp. And yes, George Washington, America's first president, leader of the revolution that gave birth to our freedoms, and lifelong hemp farmer, advised his young nation: "Make the most of the hemp seed. Sow it everywhere."

Imagine trying to explain to those two patriots that the United States now outlaws hemp production. And why? Officially, America's drug warriors fear that farmers will hide pot plants in their fields, using the look-alike hemp plants to cover up a major marijuana operation. But as anyone who's ever actually *grown* marijuana can tell you, a field of low-THC hemp would be about the last place on Earth you'd want to hide your lovely, all-female, high-THC marijuana. Just as soon as your girls started to bud, the male plants among the hemp would have a "field day" fertilizing all those virginal ladies, instantly turning your weed into seed. The hemp plants might be proud papas, but from the smoker's point of view, your (very expensive) garden just got ruined!

As we all know by now, however, making sense and the War on Drugs don't exactly go hand in hand. As far back as 1937, when hemp was outlawed via the Marijuana Tax Act, the powers that be saw an opportunity to protect their interests by creating confusion between hemp and smokable cannabis.

William Randolph Hearst not only owned the newspapers in those days, he also owned the paper mills, and didn't like the idea of his wood pulp competing against hemp paper. The powerful Dupont family had also just developed a synthetic rope material that was poised to replace the hemp-fiber rope in wide use. And the oil barons were threatened by hemp's potential as a competing source of fuel for the rapidly growing automobile industry. Together, these powerful interests launched a media and lobbying campaign that convinced Congress to condemn hardworking hemp right alongside its decidedly more laid-back cousin, marijuana. Up until that moment, hemp had been universally revered since ancient times for its many uses, with a boom in global production starting in the 18th century, when the age of shipping was powered by sails and rope made of hemp.

Today, hemp seed provides snacking stoners with a perfectly balanced blend of essential fatty acids ("phatty acids" if you must), which explains why hemp has found a home in the health food store, despite unsuccessful DEA attempts to classify hemp foods as Schedule I drugs, and ban them from the marketplace.

And don't forget, the federal government once admitted they were all wrong about hemp. During World War II, less than a decade after cultivation was prohibited, the War Department produced a short film titled *Hemp for Victory!* that encouraged America's farmers to plant hemp as their contribution to defeating the Nazis. "Hemp for mooring ships; hemp for tow lines; hemp for tackle and gear; hemp for countless naval uses both on ship and shore. . . . Hemp for victory!" the film concludes, after a lovely recap of the history of hemp extolling the many virtues of the plant for the war effort.

After the Allied victory in World War II, however, hemp fell back out of favor and the film remained buried in obscurity so deep that the government denied its very existence up until 1989, when researcher Jack Herer helped unearth a copy. Much like *Reefer Madness*, *Hemp for Victory!* revealed government hypocrisy and hysteria in an amusing way, and along with Herer's thoroughly researched book *The Emperor Wears No Clothes!*, helped launch a modern movement seeking to re-legalize the incredibly beneficial hemp plant.

Meanwhile, on the Pine Ridge Indian Reservation in South Dakota, the Lakota aren't waiting around for any change in the law. In 2000, they began planting hemp on their tribal lands, enduring the federal agents who showed up each year to raid the reservation at gunpoint and seize the crop. Suing to stop the raids, Alex White Plume, who planted the hemp, declared that he had approval from the tribal council, and pointed to the Fort Laramie Treaty of 1868, which encouraged Native Americans to farm their land. Although a federal court ruled that White Plume must cease cultivation, hemp continues to flourish on the Pine Ridge Reservation, growing wild from seeds spread across the land when the authorities dragged the previous crops away. Each autumn, the Lakota harvest these plants to make official tribal merchandise, including hemp paper for original artwork. "This hemp is more than just a crop to sell," White Plume told *High Times*. "We've prayed

Last year, the federal government devoted tons of your tax dollars to eradicating over 240 million feral hemp plants— better known as ditchweed.

over these crops and done ceremonies. This hemp represents our sovereignty, our ability to live our lives and use our land as we see fit."

THE WAR ON DITCHWEED

Want another reason to resent the federal government? How about this: They're spending your hard-earned tax dollars on ditchweed, and you don't even get to sample the goods. (Not that you'd want to anyway, but that's not the point.)

According to the DEA (now there's a name you can trust), in 2003, the agency's Domestic Cannabis Eradication/Suppression Program destroyed 247 million marijuana plants, which sounds like an impressive "victory" in the War on Drugs, until you read a bit more closely and discover that 243 million (around 99 percent) of those plants were actually feral hemp. Commonly called ditchweed, the DEA defines feral hemp as "wild, scattered marijuana plants [with] no evidence of planting, fertilizing, or tending," which, unlike cultivated marijuana, contain virtually no detectable levels of THC. Many of these wild hemp plots are descended from the U.S. government–subsidized crops planted during World War II.

By the way, Illinois, henceforth known as the Ditchweed Capital of America, led all states in feral hemp production.

THE HISTORY OF HASHISH

Like the cannabis plant it's derived from, hashish originated in Central Asia, and spread out across the globe. Hash, as it's more commonly known stateside, is made by collecting and compressing together *trichomes*, tiny oil–filled sacks attached to the thin hairs found on mature female cannabis plants. Designed to attract and capture the pollen of the male marijuana plant, these sticky, resinous trichomes contain an abundance of THC, cannabinoids, and other uplifting goodies. Separate the trichomes from the plant, smoosh them together into a smokeable substance, and you get a purer, portable, and more potent form of cannabis, capable of withstanding the extreme climates of traditional hashmaking hotspots such as Afghanistan, Pakistan, Nepal, Morocco, and Egypt.

For over a thousand years, the *indicas* indigenous to these regions have been selectively bred for better hash making, resulting in hearty, "crystal"-covered cannabis bushes sometimes called "hash plants." Through time-honored practices, these very special plants yield enough hashish to service both local demand and a worldwide market that's been growing rapidly since the '60s.

Traditional hash making includes several methods of extraction that produce varying grades of end product. In the oldest practice, a collector simply walks through the still-budding fields of cannabis, rubbing the plants by hand and rolling the resin (or *charas*) that collects into balls. After harvesting and drying, the same buds can later be shaken over screens, beaten against carpets, and pushed through sieves of varying size to filter out the rest of the trichomes from the surrounding plant matter.

The best hashish is a black, brown, or blond color, depending on the strain of pot used and the method of extraction. Hash with a green tint contains large amounts of plant matter, which dilutes its potency and flavor. Hash that's gone stale will become brittle and lose its fragrance.

In 2004, the United Nations' first Cannabis Survey revealed that 134,000 hectares of marijuana had been cultivated in Morocco in the previous year, yielding 42 percent of the world's hashish, and establishing the famous Rif Mountains as the leading international region in the production and export of hashish. Cannabis cultivation in

Morocco dates back to the arrival of Arab invaders in the 4th century, and has survived countless sultans, kings, and even Spanish rule.

TOP: *Freshly harvested herb slowly dries in Ketama, Morocco.*
ABOVE: *The best hashish appears black, brown, or blond, depending on the strain of pot used and the method of extraction.*

Various grades of homemade "bubble" hash, all produced via the modern water extraction technque.

According to the United Nations survey, the best Moroccan hash peaks at around 20 percent THC. Like fine wine, however, not just potency, but also factors such as flavor, aroma, and quality of high come into play when appreciating tradition-ally produced hashish. So if what you really desire is to just get rippin' stoned, you might want to try some hash made by the more modern method known as water extraction.

Once upon a time, marijuana growers used to make midnight runs out into the woods to get rid of the pounds of telltale fan leaves they'd trimmed off their prize buds following a big harvest. These farmers knew the leaves contained THC, but in amounts so small nobody wanted to smoke them. Nowadays, through the magic of water extraction, most growers turn that incriminating trash into homemade hash that's purer and more potent than all but the very best imports.

How do they do it? Dig this: The resinous trichomes that hold all that THC are oil based, while the excess plant matter surrounding them is water based. Oil and water do not mix. So first, submerge your ground-up marijuana leaves in water—preferably ice water, as that will make the trichomes more brittle and thus easier to break off. Thoroughly agitate the herb and ice water until the oil and water separation is complete, then run it through a series of fine-mesh screens small enough to trap the broken-off trichomes float-ing in the water. Collect this resin off the screens, compress it with your fingers into flat discs, and let the discs dry overnight. Several ready-made sys-tems are available to facilitate this process, or you can always make your own. Either way, you'll wake up the next morning and start the day off right with a deliciously potent and ass-kickingly power-ful hashish that's so full of oily trichomes it will probably bubble up when you touch it with your lighter—hence the term "bubble hash." In fact, the best "ice" hashes reach such high potencies that they've earned their own category in the *High Times* Cannabis Cup, which awards one prize for hashish imported from traditional hash-producing nations, and another for Amsterdam's homemade "bubble hash." (As if judging two dozen varieties of hashish in just under a week wasn't confusing enough . . . not that we're complaining!)

SOIL VS. HYDRO

Hydro is short for hydroponics, the science of growing plants without soil, which dates back at least as far as the famed Hanging Gardens of Babylon. During World War II, U.S. soldiers grew hydro vegetables to help sustain the war effort on barren islands in the Pacific, where traditional farming wasn't possible. And someday, hydroponic farming could provide a way to sustain life in outer space.

But for our purposes, it's mostly a way to grow some killer weed. When done correctly, hydroponic gardening can be significantly more efficient than soil, providing plants with an exacting diet of essential nutrients and thus yielding faster-growing, heavier harvests, but hydro's also far less forgiving than soil. Make a mistake, and like a downhill skier who catches an edge, it will be difficult to regain control.

For first-time growers, *High Times* generally recommends starting with soil to get your roots wet, but if you've got easy access to a hydroponics system and enjoy tinkering with gadgets, don't be afraid to try hydro your first time out.

Top: *Soil gardens require less attention and expertise than hydroponics.* Above: *Hydroponic growing uses inert mediums like rock wool, expanded clay or coco-peat in place of soil.*

TOP: *Devote your time and energy to ganja gardening, and this could be you!* ABOVE: *Cannabis seedlings grow quickly if given proper love and attention.*

THE PERFECT ROOMMATE *Devote your basement, attic, bedroom, or closet to cultivating cannabis, and those blessed pot plants will pay a lot more than their half of the rent*

For an experienced marijuana horticulturist, constructing a fully functioning grow room accommodating up to sixty plants will take less than a day, once all of the required components and materials have been assembled. Building the grow room, however, is really just the beginning. In an outdoor garden, Mother Nature takes care of most of the plant's needs, but indoors, it's up to the grower to provide light, air, water, and nutrients, consistently and in the proper amounts. Remember, "playing God" in your garden gives you the power to grow outstanding ganja, but only if you give your grass all the love and attention it deserves.

Here's what you need to get started.

🍁 SEEDS OR CLONES

Whether you start with seeds or cuttings from a mother plant, try to get the best genetics possible, and make sure you're growing a strain of cannabis bred for indoor gardens. The more you know about the strain the better, including its strengths and weaknesses, how tall it usually stretches, how much it yields, and how many weeks it will flower before the buds peak.

🍁 STRUCTURE

Find a space with enough room for your plants and equipment, adequate electricity to run high-intensity lights, ceilings at least five feet tall, and easy access to a faucet. Enclose this grow space and cover the walls, floor, and ceiling with a strong, reflective material like white visqueen plastic. Make sure no light escapes from the grow room, that it's completely concealed, and preferably behind a locked door.

☙ AIR

The grow room should be constantly monitored for proper temperature and humidity. Without adequate ventilation and circulation, the air inside indoor grow rooms will quickly grow too warm and too humid to sustain optimal growth. In fact, all of the air inside an indoor grow room should be replaced every five minutes.

Air should also circulate around the room so that the individual leaves on each pot plant flutter as if in a breeze. This promotes the exchange of CO_2 and oxygen essential to photosynthesis. Lastly, a filtration system must be installed to clean the discharge air of marijuana's distinct aroma before it exits the grow room.

☙ LIGHTS

Indoor marijuana gardens require high-intensity grow lights of the proper spectrum for cannabis. For most operations, 600-watt high-pressure sodium lights tend to be the most efficient, but you'll have to calculate your own needs based on the size of your garden, the number of plants, the number of lights, and available vertical height.

Hang your lights as close to the plants as possible without overheating them, testing by placing your palm at the level of the canopy. If it's too hot to comfortably keep your hand there, then it's too hot for the plants, and you need to raise your lights.

Up to a hundred small plants can fit under a single 400-watt light, but they will need significantly more space as they grow taller.

Make sure you follow all applicable electrical codes when installing and using high-intensity lights, and only use lights in perfect working order. Never steal electricity to power a grow room, as this is a common way growers get caught.

☙ GROWING MEDIUM

Whether you grow in soil or hydroponically, something will have to hold your plants in place while providing the roots with the nutrients they need to sustain rapid growth. In soil gardens, this process works much as it does outdoors, except the grower mixes the soil to ideal proportions before planting and then maintains total control over water and nutrients. These gardens require high-quality potting soil and fertilizers, plus containers of varying sizes to accommodate all stages of growth.

In hydroponic gardens, an inorganic growing medium such as rock wool, coco fiber, or expanded clay tablets takes the place of soil. Your local hydroponics store will have various types of systems available, from extremely automated to simple do-it-yourself setups that can be easily put together with some materials from the hardware store.

THE GOOD BOOK

Hopefully this humble little handbook has helped answer a few simple cultivation questions, like *Why grow herb indoors?* and *What's the deal with all*

ABOVE: *Jorge Cervantes,* High Times *cultivation expert, the world's most trusted ganja guide, and the best-selling author of* Marijuana Horticulture. OPPOSITE: *Drying cannabis properly takes 7–10 days, and the waiting is definitely the hardest part.*

those different names? But someday, if you decide to take the next step and plant a pot garden of your very own, you'll have questions such as *What are the ideal humidity and PH levels for a vegetative plant in a top-feed hydro unit?* and *Which organic fertilizer releases the highest levels of nitrogen during flowering?* That's when it's time to call in Jorge Cervantes, best-selling author, *High Times* cultivation expert, and the world's most trusted ganja guide.

The first and most important thing every marijuana farmer needs, whether you're growing indoors or outdoors, hydroponically or in soil, is access to accurate information, and you can't do better than Jorge's *Marijuana Horticulture*

(also known as "The Pot Grower's Bible") and his two *Ultimate Grow* DVDs from *High Times*.

Since 1983, Jorge's sold over five hundred thousand copies of his books, and now he's also filmed two DVDs' worth of garden visits that will show you exactly what he's been writing about all these years. So don't do anything in your garden until you've consulted with Jorge, because if you're going to invest your precious time, money, and energy into growing weed, you really should know what the hell you're doing first.

HOW TO HAVE A HEAVY HARVEST

"Holy *frijole*, my plants have gotten huge. I remember when they were just little clones, fresh clipped from their mother plant, still struggling to take root . . . and now, look at these lovely, lovely ladies. They grow up so fast, *sniffle, sniffle*."

Nothing's harder than knowing when to harvest. On the one hand, you can't wait to start smoking all that amazing marijuana, and on the other, you've grown so attached to your beautiful garden that you can barely bring yourself to cut the cord. But it must be done before the buds go past their peak, and the optimal harvesting window only stays open for about five days.

Gauge the ripeness of your ganja by examining the resin glands, which change color as they mature. For the best view, use a magnifying glass, jeweler's loupe, or even a hand-held microscope. As resinous trichomes approach their peak, they will

Beware of Dog—especially if you plan on stealing any of his owner's ganja.

start off clear, turn a translucent milky white, and finally darken to amber. Most growers try to harvest at the first sign of fully mature, amber trichomes.

About two weeks before harvest, flush out your garden with plenty of water to remove any excess fertilizer and then stop watering two days before harvest so the plants will dry more quickly once you cut them. For optimal THC levels, always harvest in the morning.

Beware: Your girls will never smell sweeter or more pungent than at harvest time, an otherwise pleasing aroma that unfortunately can be over-powering enough to alert the neighbors to what you've been doing down in your basement over the past few months. So plan your harvest as care-fully as your planting, keeping in mind you'll need to dry, trim, and cure all those buds before you smoke a single joint.

First, figure out where you can securely hang up your harvest *before* you chop it down, and install an air filter if the smell poses a problem. The dry-ing room should be cool and dark, with good air circulation and temperatures below 70 degrees Fahrenheit. Never dry plants in the same room where you're growing them.

Once you've got your drying room ready, cut the main stem at the bottom of each fully mature plant with sharp clippers and then use scissors to trim off the largest branches and fan leaves while the plants are still wet. Save the trimmed leaves to make water–extraction hash (see page 194), and hang the buds upside down from the stems for five to seven days to dry. Don't put fresh buds in the microwave, in direct sunlight, or even point a fan at them, as these "quick dry" methods all degrade the quality of the cannabis you worked so hard to grow.

Once the stems snap cleanly when bent, you can take them down and trim off any remaining leaves. Work over a silkscreen or kief catcher so you can collect the fallen resin and press it into hash. High-quality "scissor hash" will also collect as you trim, which makes the sometimes pains-taking manicuring process a lot more fun, not to mention helps you resist the temptation to start smoking all those sweet buds before they're cured.

Curing—the process of slowly leaching the last traces of moisture out of "dry" buds—protects the THC and other cannabinoids from breaking down too quickly during storage, and also prevents mold. Properly cured herb is more potent and flavorful, and produces a far smoother smoke.

Place your buds in an airtight glass container, piling in as many as possible without damaging them. Moisture will evaporate into the air trapped in the jar, slowly drying the buds from the inside out. Periodically open the jar and turn the buds over to release this moisture and allow more sweating. Check the buds several times per day until they're perfectly and evenly dry.

And then, yes—you can finally roll some up and get higher than a motherfucker. It will be all the more special because you waited.

SECURITY CHECK

No matter how you work it, growing marijuana involves taking a chance, but you can minimize the risks by taking proper precautions in and around your garden. Keep your home tidy and in good repair, rake the yard, shovel the sidewalk, and be polite to the neighbors, without making friends. No wild parties or other excuses for the police to visit. Drive a street-legal car and pay your bills on time. Have all of the electrical work in your grow room up to code and include a fire extinguisher. Make sure no light, smell, or sound escapes from your grow room, and never have grow-related equipment mailed to your home address. Never store incriminating materials in plain sight or throw them out at the curb. Always pay cash at the grow store, visit as infrequently as possible, and borrow a non-growing buddy's car to make the trip. Most important, never sell weed from the same location as your garden, and never,

ever tell anyone what you're up to unless they need to know.

The most successful growers, who harvest crop after crop without incident, are the ones you'd never suspect, and that's exactly why they're so successful.

MEET MARY JANE *From Northern Lights to Panama Red, get to know the most famous herb strains of all time*

Sit down to dinner at a five-star French restaurant, and a sommelier will gladly help you select a bottle of wine. That's the whole job, knowing a lot about wine. Which, naturally, means drinking a lot of wine.

Now wouldn't it be great if they had that job for weed? Of course, there's a lot to know, so you'd have to be prepared to undertake some intensive study. Let's start with the basics: Much the same way many fine wines are named for the place where the variety of grape originated (Chablis, Shiraz, Beaujolais), many of the best old-school smokes were also named in honor of their homelands, including Acapulco Gold, Maui Wowie, and Panama Red. The entire line of Kush strains takes its name from the Kush Mountains in Afghanistan.

So how did we go from that to Purple Crunch-berry Holy Smokes? You take the best of what grew up naturally all around the world, known as "land race" strains, and start cross-pollinating them with each other. Some of the resulting hybrids will turn purple just before harvest. Some will taste like Crunchberries. Some will make you see God. And if you keep crossing long enough, you'll finally find one that will do all three.

Both amateur and professional seed breeders create new strains all the time, naming the best ones and spreading them out across the world by sharing (or selling) seeds and clones. So yes, all those weird names do actually relate to distinctly different plants, but there's also an awful lot of jive talking that goes on, particularly by unscrupulous dealers looking to cash in on some strain's star appeal.

So if a reefer man ever hands you Brown Schwag and tells you it's Strawberry Cough, definitely consult with your weed sommelier before making the deal.

ABOVE: *According to legend, G-13 originated in the federal government's Marijuana Research Facility at the University of Mississippi* OPPOSITE: *Few of the world's natural wonders compare to beholding a magnificent display of Northern Lights.*

PANAMA RED

Made famous by the New Riders of the Purple Sage song of the same name, Panama Red is a powerful *sativa* named for its red hairs. Not commercially available since the '80s (at least outside Panama), the famous Red lends its genetics to some of today's top strains, including Love Potion #1, a winner at the 2005 Cannabis Cup.

NORTHERN LIGHTS X HAZE

Developed by Amsterdam seed breeders, this hybrid combines Northern Lights, an easy-to-grow, abundantly yielding *indica*, with the soaring high of Haze, a slow-growing, wispy *sativa*. The result blends the best of both worlds, yielding dense, resin-soaked buds that bring a clear, uplifting intoxication.

THAI STICK

First introduced to Americans during the Vietnam War, these buds from Thailand arrived meticulously manicured and tied to 4- to 6-inch-long slivers of bamboo.

G-13

Allegedly, G stands for "government" and 13 for M, the thirteenth letter of the alphabet. Put them together, and you've got G-13, government marijuana, purportedly pinched from the federal Marijuana Research Facility at the University of Mississippi. Whether you believe the story or not, this pure *indica* unleashes a powerful high and an intense, musky flavor.

CANNABIS EVOLUTION:
30 YEARS OF *HIGH TIMES'* BEST BUDS

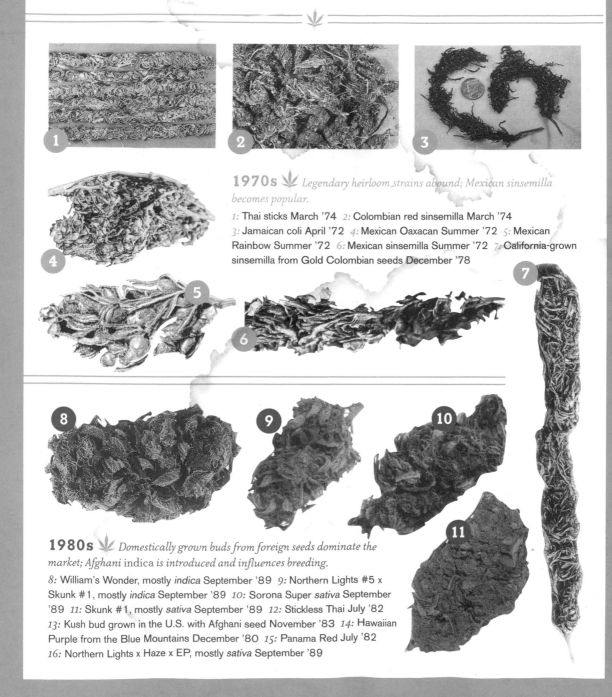

1970s 🌿 *Legendary heirloom strains abound; Mexican sinsemilla becomes popular.*

1: Thai sticks March '74 *2:* Colombian red sinsemilla March '74 *3:* Jamaican coli April '72 *4:* Mexican Oaxacan Summer '72 *5:* Mexican Rainbow Summer '72 *6:* Mexican sinsemilla Summer '72 *7:* California-grown sinsemilla from Gold Colombian seeds December '78

1980s 🌿 *Domestically grown buds from foreign seeds dominate the market; Afghani indica is introduced and influences breeding.*

8: William's Wonder, mostly *indica* September '89 *9:* Northern Lights #5 x Skunk #1, mostly *indica* September '89 *10:* Sorona Super *sativa* September '89 *11:* Skunk #1, mostly *sativa* September '89 *12:* Stickless Thai July '82 *13:* Kush bud grown in the U.S. with Afghani seed November '83 *14:* Hawaiian Purple from the Blue Mountains December '80 *15:* Panama Red July '82 *16:* Northern Lights x Haze x EP, mostly *sativa* September '89

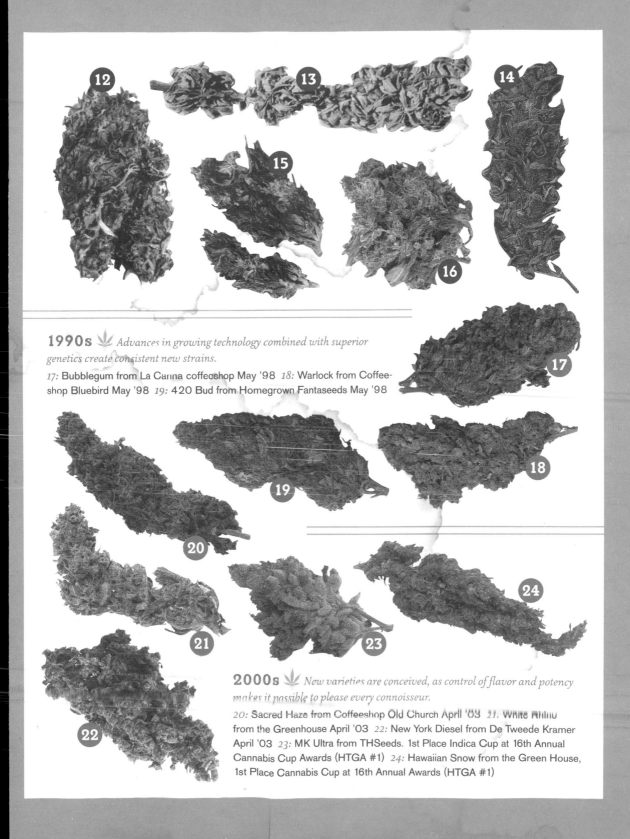

1990s 🍁 *Advances in growing technology combined with superior genetics create consistent new strains.*

17: Bubblegum from La Canna coffeeshop May '98 *18:* Warlock from Coffeeshop Bluebird May '98 *19:* 420 Bud from Homegrown Fantaseeds May '98

2000s 🍁 *New varieties are conceived, as control of flavor and potency makes it possible to please every connoisseur.*

20: Sacred Haze from Coffeeshop Old Church April '03 *21:* White Rhino from the Greenhouse April '03 *22:* New York Diesel from De Tweede Kramer April '03 *23:* MK Ultra from THSeeds. 1st Place Indica Cup at 16th Annual Cannabis Cup Awards (HTGA #1) *24:* Hawaiian Snow from the Green House, 1st Place Cannabis Cup at 16th Annual Awards (HTGA #1)

ACKNOWLEDGMENTS

The author wishes to acknowledge the efforts of countless coconspirators, without whom this book would not be possible. First, and foremost, *High Times* founder Tom Forcade, and all the staff, past and present, at the world's most notorious magazine. Many brilliant photographers contributed, particularly Andre Grossman, MG Imaging, Brian Jahn, Danny Danko, Dan Skye, and Aaron Strebs. HT Production Director Elise McDonough scoured the HT archives to find our best photos.

Special thanks to Jorge Cervantes, Robert Platshorn, Kris Krane, Mason Tvert, Allen St. Pierre, Keith Stroup, Rick Cusick, Captain Zero, Mike Clattenburg, the Namaste Center for Sustainable Ganja Farming and the kind people of Punta Mona.

This book owes its life to the consistent efforts of Steve Mockus, Kim Romero, Brooke Johnson, Laura Bagnato, Erin Thacker, Lisa Anne Logan, April Whitney, Molly Jones, and Doug Ogan at Chronicle Books, and my fantastic agent, Alex Glass at Trident Media Group.

CREDITS